OVERTIME
Is Our Time!

The Inside Story of the Maryland Terps'
2006 National Championship

By Chris King with Coach Brenda Frese

ISBN 0-9788082-0-7

Printed in the United States

First edition

For additional copies, call 1-800-932-4557 or email OTisourtime@aol.com

Website: OvertimeIsOurTime.com

Cover design by Dennis Tuttle, and graphics consultation by Paul Compton.
Book design by American Sports Media, Rochester, N.Y.
Front cover photo by Getty Images. Back cover and author photos by Bill Vaughan

Photos courtesy Bill Vaughan — pages 1, 9, 25, 35, 45, 55, 67, 83, 89, 90, 92, 93,
94, 105, 121, 131, 137, 149, 159, 171. Photos courtesy Mark Thomas — pages 91,
95, 96, 183. Photos courtesy Frese family — pages 96, 112. Photo courtesy Michael
Frantel — page 137.

To Amy and Cooper, who make every day a great one.
— Chris

ACKNOWLEDGMENTS

Writing a book is a daunting task and not one successfully accomplished by a single individual. Overtime Is Our Time is a byproduct of the hard work and selflessness of many people, and I would like to thank the following for their contributions.

Brenda Frese and the Maryland Terrapins were more accessible and pleasant to deal with than could have been reasonably expected. The willingness of Frese, her coaching staff and players to candidly discuss the season — its highs and occasional lows — were at the heart of the book's development. Brenda Frese, Joanna Bernabei, Erica Floyd and Jeff Walz gave of their time on multiple occasions, despite incredibly busy schedules.

Maryland's players — Marissa Coleman, Shay Doron, Laura Harper, Crystal Langhorne, Ashleigh Newman, Aurelie Noirez, Jade Perry, Kristi Toliver and Sa'de Wiley-Gatewood — were well spoken advocates, not just for the Maryland basketball team but the university, making this project much easier to undertake.

It takes a team of people to nurture a book from conception to printing, and the coach of this squad was Rick Snider, who deserves a special thanks.

Thank you to Mark Pearson, who provided much information and assistance in arranging many of the meetings that made this book a reality. Just as he plays a vital, but mostly anonymous, role in the team's day-to-day activities, Mark was of tremendous assistance to me.

Mark Thomas was always available to field a question or relay a story, many of which are part of the narrative.

I owe a debt of gratitude to Keith Cavanaugh, who knows all things Maryland athletics, and gave me the opportunity to join the Terrapin Times team. Keith is the genesis of the book and provided feedback and encouragement throughout the process.

Thank you to Natalia Ciccone, the team's media relations contact, who answered all questions, large and small.

To Dick Heller and Megan Snider, who made this book eminently more readable, thanks for your work. A special thanks to cover designer Dennis Tuttle and book designer American Sports Media.

Many deserve acknowledgement for their support, including Mike Ashley, who once prodded a young man more interested in a good time than hard work. Mike has grown from mentor to friend, though still dispensing invaluable advice.

To my parents Robert and Diane King, thanks for everything.

Thanks to Amy and Cooper for their patience and understanding during the process, and the pleasure they bring to my life.

—Chris King

ACKNOWLEDGMENTS

Winning a National Championship does not define me. For me, it is about the kids and the relationships. Truthfully, I always dreamed of getting a team to the Final Four. Every year, I sat in the stands, watching and wondering what it would be like. So imagine how I felt the night before our game that could advance our team to our first Final Four, when I found myself in New Mexico, kneeling on a hotel bathroom floor and hunched over a toilet. A wicked stomach virus worked its way through our team and it could not have come at a worse time. Everything we'd worked for was in jeopardy of going down the drain. Somehow, our kids found a way to "gut it out," winning our fifth overtime game of the year and getting us to Boston. Anybody interested in losing a few quick pounds, consult us about the "Albuquerque Diet."

That performance was one of our team's defining moments in 2005-06. Imagine going 6-0 in overtime against great competition, with all six games on the road and the biggest of the bunch being for the National Championship. Age truly was just a number for this young team that was fearless, driven and not surprised by what it accomplished.

This season was special and I want to thank everyone who was involved. From my players, to our support personnel, to my entire coaching staff (Jeff Walz, Erica Floyd, Joanna Bernabei and Mark Pearson) who truly lined up as one all season long. We were a united front that took everyone's best shots, but would not be broken.

To my husband, Mark Thomas, what a ride to receive two rings in less than a year! I am so fortunate to have found my best friend and to experience everything with you. Thank you for helping me to achieve balance in my life. Your loving family is now my family and has made Maryland truly feel like home.

To my dad and mom (Bill and Donna Frese) — thank you for instilling and displaying a work ethic every single day. You supported me every step of the way and helped me become who I am. To my brother (Jeff) and sisters (Deb, Cindy, Marsha and Stacy), I couldn't ask for a better team to go through life with! Thank you for always keeping me grounded and level headed.

To my Athletics Director Dr. Deborah Yow — you are the best in the business. From the day I stepped on campus, we've shared the same passion for the program. I admire and appreciate what you have accomplished in a male dominated world. You've done so much for this school, it would be a travesty if the University of Maryland does not name something on campus in your honor.

To the parents of our players — thank you for trusting me with your daughters. I know how precious they are to you and I share your desire for them to have the best experience possible. They wouldn't be the champions they are today without your influence.

Finally, thanks to everyone who supported or took an interest in our team. The season that is recapped in this book (thanks Chris King and Keith Cavanaugh) was a glorious ride. I hope you enjoy reliving it as much as we do.

— Brenda Frese

CONTENTS

1. "Your Life Is Going to Change" 1

2. From Budapest to College Park 9

3. A Young Pup Bites 25

4. Almost Paradise 35

5. "My Stretch of Going Insane" 45

6. "I'm Going to Die for a Recruit" 55

7. "We Should Thank Duke" 67

8. "Boston '06" 83

9. Assistant Coaches 105

10. First Family of Cedar Rapids Athletics 113

11. "I'm a Team Player" 121

12. 'EKUD' 131

13. The Journey Begins 137

14. Dead Women Walking 149

15. Final Four 159

16. "I Knew She was Going to Shoot the Ball" ...171

17. A Budding Super Power? 183

Chapter 1

"Your Life Is Going to Change"

"Are we fired up or what? We are playing the No. 1 team in the country, again," Maryland coach Brenda Frese said to her squad. "This is why you play basketball. This is what you are living for. This is why you practice — to be in match-ups like this."

Frese and her Terrapins were in the bowels of Carmichael Auditorium, the venerable building the North Carolina women call home, preparing to face the undefeated and top-ranked Tar Heels on Feb. 9, 2006. As she delivered her pregame talk, the players sat pensively on wooden benches, some staring straight ahead, others almost looking through a tile floor installed decades before their birth. Behind Frese, the message on the chalkboard read, "The stars come out tonight," a point the young coach wanted to emphasize.

Frese started to smile as she reached into the pocket of her black suit pants, pulling out a package of Starburst candy.

"Tonight is our night and sitting in this locker room are a bunch of stars," she said. "There are a lot of different flavors here and we are going to burst out with a lot of energy, but what you don't realize is, your life is going to change after tonight. Not only are you going to win this game, you are going to burst onto the national scene. Let's go get it done."

The players smiled as Frese handed each one a piece of the candy — a hokey gesture that nonetheless lightened the mood. It was classic Frese. Moments before a big game, her squad had a laugh, at least a little bit of it at her expense, but there was a great measure of truth to what she was telling them — and each player in the room knew it.

From the moment Frese stepped on Maryland's campus in April 2002, she made the Terps a player on the national recruiting scene. Each of her first three classes was ranked among the top 10 nationally.

Maryland was assembling a roster with championship talent, and everybody knew it. The question facing the Terps was whether a team starting one junior, two sophomores and two freshmen had the experience and emotional maturity to compete with powerhouses Connecticut, Tennessee, Stanford, Duke and, yes, North Carolina.

Maryland arrived in Chapel Hill with a 21-2 record and a seven-game winning streak, the only losses to Tennessee and Duke, with neither ranked lower than No. 2 when they beat the Terps. But Maryland wasn't playing up to its potential, and the Terps were well aware of what was being said about them.

The team's record indicated that youth wasn't a problem, but as the victories mounted, the Terps' play was dissected and people began finding weaknesses. It was no longer enough for them merely to win. In the seven victories before the North Carolina game, the Terps went into overtime twice and won two other games by eight points or less, mostly against competition they were expected to defeat with relative ease. Despite being ranked No. 6 in the country, Maryland was beginning to hear more about what it wasn't than what it was. With each narrow escape, the talk grew louder: The Terps are too young, they don't play defense or — everybody's favorite — they aren't ready to contend for a national championship this season.

Kristi Toliver, always among the first Terrapins to emerge from the locker room for pregame shooting, couldn't wait to get on the Carmichael floor. The daughter of a 17-year National Basketball Association referee, Toliver grew up around the NBA despite living in Harrisonburg, Va., a quaint town in the heart of the Shenandoah Valley. Her father George Toliver had taken her to countless games over the years, including a trip to the 1993 NBA All-Star Game in Salt Lake City, Utah, where she sat in front of Michael Jordan's parents. At the age of six, Toliver already knew she wanted to "Be Like Mike," as the line in a famous commercial jingle said.

By game's end, Toliver was begging Jordan's parents to help her get an autograph from her idol. Unable to get the coveted signature in Salt Lake City, she left her address with Deloris Jordan. A few weeks later, Toliver received a package in the mail that included a couple of photos signed by Michael Jordan and a personal note from Deloris. Toliver, who was beyond ecstatic, still keeps the treasured photos and note at her Harrisonburg home.

As she headed onto the floor at Carmichael, Toliver, a freshman, was well aware of who used to call the court home. The one thing going through her mind was, "I'm in MJ's gym." Toliver was born nearly two years after Jordan left North Carolina, but she knew his history, and time hadn't lessened her admiration for the player many regard as the greatest ever to play the game.

She didn't have long to daydream about Jordan's days in Chapel Hill, because the Terrapins couldn't have picked a more difficult opponent to "burst" out against. Jordan had long since left Carmichael, but the building's current tenant, the North Carolina women, were ranked No. 1 in the nation at 22-0 and were prohibitive favorites.

When the game started, Maryland seemed closer to collapsing than bursting out. The Terps turned the ball over 15 times in the first 20 minutes, and North Carolina seemed to corral every loose ball. Playing in front of 6,417 fans mostly dressed in baby blue, Maryland was fortunate to be down only 46-36 at the half. The smile on Frese's face as she sent her team onto the court to start the game had long since disappeared.

"Is the pressure too much? Because right now we are choking, plain and simple," she said to her team in a stern but even voice at the half. "What I don't understand is, you work just as hard as Carolina, if not harder. Why do you give up so easily? How are you not fired the hell up? You have 20 minutes to go out and play great basketball. We are just as talented as this group."

Despite her relative calm, Frese was angry. Losing isn't an unpardonable sin in her view, but playing timidly is another matter. By the end of her halftime talk, Frese's voice was reaching a crescendo, and the players responded with emotion of their own.

In a business where it's easy for coaches to focus on the negative, Frese prefers to deliver a positive message, even when circumstances dictate she be tougher on players. The Terps had 20 minutes to erase a 10-point deficit, and Frese made it abundantly clear her team was up to the task.

Maryland competed fiercely in the second half, but with the Tar Heels leading 73-60 and just 7:35 remaining, North Carolina appeared en route to another win. Led by Marissa Coleman and Shay Doron, who scored seven straight Maryland points during one stretch, the Terps clawed their way back. With 15 seconds left, Maryland got the chance it had been waiting for. Trailing 82-80, the Terps were forced to foul Ivory Latta, North Carolina's star. An 85 percent free throw shooter, Latta missed the second attempt, leaving the score 83-80 and giving Maryland a chance to tie.

Frese signaled for a timeout with 10 seconds remaining and called a play for Doron to take the potential game-tying shot. Doron took the inbounds pass and launched a three-pointer from straight away that hit the back of the rim, but neither team could control the rebound. As the ball emerged from a scrum around the basket, Ashleigh Newman, 0-for-8 shooting to that point, chased it down at least 25 feet from the basket and heaved up a shot from the right wing.

As the ball approached the rim, the red neon light signifying the end of regulation lit up the backboard, but Newman's shot was true from the moment it left her hand. With the backboard light still on and the buzzer sounding, the ball swished through the net to tie the game at 83-83. North Carolina's players and fans were stunned as the young interlopers from College Park mobbed Newman at midcourt.

Maryland was going into overtime for the fourth time in 10 games, and the Terps had yet to lose. With adrenaline still coursing through the huddle, Frese reminded her players of what they had done to battle back from the second-half deficit.

"We got back in this game because we got every loose ball," she said, the intensity in her voice audible to everyone. "The hustle plays are ours!"

As Frese broke the huddle, a player yelled, "Overtime is what?"

"Our time!" the team responded.

The Terps seized control in the opening possessions of overtime, jumping out to an 88-83 lead just over a minute into the extra session. North Carolina, fighting to protect its No. 1 ranking, an undefeated season, and a 30-game home win streak, rallied within 96-95 and then fouled Toliver, sending her to the line in the type of pressure situation Jordan had built his legend on with 17 seconds left. She drained two free throws to push the Terps lead to 98-95, but the Tar Heels still had an opportunity for their own last-second heroics.

Though Camille Little and Latta launched three-point attempts in the final five seconds, both were off target. North Carolina fans screamed for a foul after Latta's attempt, but their cries went unanswered. The Terps escaped with a 98-95 road win, sending America's last unbeaten team to defeat.

The Maryland locker room after the game was as animated as it had been all season. Players yelled, posed, preened, punched fists in the air and made cell phone calls to relay news of the victory to parents and friends. In the middle of all the hooting and hollering, Doron gleefully issued one of the night's sweetest proclamations: The Terps had earned dessert, touching off another eruption from her teammates.

In an effort to improve her team's eating habits, Frese, at the behest of strength and conditioning coach Corliss Fingers, eliminated dessert as part of the team's travel meals unless they earned it. The Terps hadn't enjoyed dessert all season, but they more than deserved the post-meal treat of their choice on this night.

Amid the celebration, Coleman quieted the joyous yells of her teammates to apologize. In the second half, with Maryland still fighting to get back in the game and the team huddled around the foul line during a break in the action, Coleman had her head turned listening to instructions from the bench. Toliver, unaware that Coleman was talking to a coach, placed her hand on the side of Coleman's face and tried to pull her into the team's huddle. Coleman pushed her arm away in anger and momentarily lost her composure. It wasn't an extraordinary blowup, particularly during a hotly contested game, but Coleman, a freshman, felt compelled to apologize. Her teammates laughed about the episode and resumed their celebration, but Coleman's conciliatory gesture revealed nearly as much about her character and that of the team as its comeback.

By their own admission, the Terps enjoyed the benefit of luck in the late stages of the game, but luck had nothing to do with the tenacity they exhibited in rallying from deficits as large as 14 points. As good teams often seem to do, Maryland put itself in position to get lucky.

Enjoying the benefits of modern technology, the team crowded around a laptop on the charter flight home watching the game, particularly Newman's shot, until the flight attendant ordered them to sit down so the plane could land at Baltimore-Washington International Airport. When their charter bus arrived at Comcast Center at 12:56 a.m., the pep band and a small group of supporters met the team, playing the school's fight song as the players departed the bus singing along.

Frese's Starburst speech suddenly seemed apropos. Maryland had indeed burst onto the national scene. The lack of live television coverage didn't prevent highlights of the game from making it to ESPN's "SportsCenter." Newman's shot sat atop ESPN's daily list of the Top 10 Plays and was replayed across the nation throughout the next 24 hours.

The Terps went to Chapel Hill believing they were a good team. They came home knowing they were a good team with the potential to be great. Just as Frese predicted before the game, their lives began to change. Students on campus started to take more notice, and critics couldn't point to their youth without acknowledging the mental fortitude, athleticism and skill needed to win at North Carolina.

Maryland's players talked of going to the Final Four and winning a national championship at the start of the season. At 22-2, the talk was beginning to look like more than youthful bravado. Newman's shot at the end of regulation changed more than the Terps and the perception of their program. On that night in Chapel Hill, the balance of power in women's college basketball made a slow, inevitable turn toward College Park.

Chapter 2

From Budapest to College Park

When Frese was introduced to the media and Maryland fans at a press conference on April 3, 2002, the Terrapins women's basketball team couldn't have been farther from the national spotlight. The third head coach in the program's history, Frese inherited a team that had gone 13-17 overall, 4-12 in ACC play and graduated five seniors.

Under coach Chris Weller, Maryland once was the league's dominant program, winning a record eight ACC titles during a 12-year stretch beginning in 1978. Weller took the Terps to their second Final Four in 1989, when they lost to Tennessee, 77-65, in the national semifinal in Tacoma, Wash.

Instead of being a milestone to build on, the Final Four appearance was as much an end as a beginning for Weller, who won 499 games in her illustrious 27-year tenure in College Park. The women's game grew exponentially after the passage of the Title IX legislation in 1972 that banned sex discrimination in education and required colleges and universities to provide women with equal access and funding. By the 1990s, the effects of Title IX were seen most clearly in the burgeoning popularity of the women's game. Schools were devoting more resources to women's basketball and were reaping rewards in terms of increased exposure and greater attendance.

But while the level of competition was rising, Maryland's program started to stagnate. After a trip to the Sweet 16 in 1992, the Terps didn't win another NCAA Tournament game until Frese's arrival. In the final 10 years of Weller's tenure, the team advanced to the NCAAs just three times, getting blown out in its first game on each occasion.

What worked in Maryland's favor when Frese came on board was the opening of the Comcast Center, a state-of-the-art facility that seats

17,950 and makes a strong argument for being the nation's finest on-campus arena, as well as giving Maryland a significant recruiting advantage in the talent-rich Washington, D.C. area.

The potential of the Maryland women's basketball program has become much more obvious in the wake of Frese's success, but it wasn't considered a top five job when she arrived. In fact, Frese's first season was the most difficult of her professional life.

Frese, then known by her married name of Brenda Oldfield, came to Maryland after one season at the University of Minnesota, where she took over a team that was 8-20 before her arrival and guided the Golden Gophers to a 22-8 mark and into the second round of the NCAA Tournament. Frese turned a Minnesota team reeling in the wake of Cheryl Littlejohn's scandal-plagued tenure into a gate attraction. The Gophers, who drew just 1,103 fans for Frese's home debut, attracted 12,142 for the regular-season home finale, and she was named Associated Press National Coach of the Year.

Frese's decision to leave Minnesota after just 10 months was the most controversial of her career. She was savaged in the Minnesota press for leaving, making her initial transition to College Park all the more difficult. Frese was going through a divorce, hence the return to her maiden name. The divorce, the difficulty of the rebuilding job and the beating she took in the Minnesota media exacted a toll. But once her staff (including sister Marsha) made the move to Maryland, she began to settle in.

The backbone of Frese's rise through the coaching ranks has been her work ethic. Whether scouting AAU games, breaking down game tape or recruiting, she has never been afraid of long work days. Given the state of the Terps program, that was fortunate.

Frese and the staff brought with her from Minnesota — assistant coaches Jeff Walz, Erica Floyd, Marsha Frese and director of basketball operations Mark Pearson — knew there wouldn't be a quick fix at Maryland like there was the year before in Minnesota. The talent wasn't there.

"Anytime you go into a new program and you bring your own philosophy and mindset, the first year is the toughest," Frese said. "Of all the rebuilding jobs I've had, this was by far the most difficult. Maryland graduated five seniors and returned two [bench] players that were going to be starting. I spent a lot of time talking to support staff trying to understand the personalities and who made [team play their top priority]."

The first year was as difficult on the court as Frese anticipated. The Terps went 10-18, including 4-12 in ACC play, and lost 11 of their last

13 games. The unquestioned low point of the season was a 101-52 shel-lacking at Duke in January, the worst loss Frese endured as a head coach.

"I remember flying back with the team questioning myself and whether I was the right coach for the program," Frese recalled. "I got a message from [Maryland athletics director] Debbie Yow, herself a for-mer coach, saying, 'Hey, I saw the score. There will come a day when we will beat Duke.' "

The message, in addition to proving prophetic, heartened Frese, but it didn't help on the court. When the Blue Devils, the ACC's standard bearer in women's basketball, made the return trip to College Park on Feb. 24, the Terps narrowed the gap to 97-55 — a loss that took place just days after Frese's divorce from Steve Oldfield was finalized.

Lacking the firepower necessary to compete in the ACC, Frese focused her energy that first year on recruiting players who could win at the highest level and creating a positive environment. The Terps didn't win consecutive games after the turn of the year, so staying positive wasn't easy. But they focused on being competitive, even if only for short stretches, and there were encouraging signs. Four of Maryland's last eight losses were by four points or less, so the team played hard throughout.

As much as anybody in the game, Frese understands that talent wins games. She dedicated as much time as possible in year one to recruiting, often leaving Walz in charge of practice while she hit the road.

Despite the challenges, Frese was out selling her dream to the nation's best players, challenging them to help her turn Maryland into a national champion. She was on the road whenever NCAA rules allowed and would take calls from recruits anytime, and her efforts were reward-ed. Frese's work on the recruiting trail that first year laid the groundwork for the team's future success.

Her first Maryland recruiting class, signed in November 2002, included Kalika France and Doron, both top 25 national recruits, and Aurelie Noirez. With her first class ranked 10th in the nation, Frese hit the road in pursuit of players in the class of 2004, one of the deepest and most talented in women's basketball history. The Terps' 10-18 record for the 2002-03 season was the first losing mark Frese had endured as an assistant or head coach, and she was determined not to let it happen again.

With high school All-Americans Doron and France in the fold, things began to change. Frese served notice that she would pursue the best recruits in the country, regardless of Maryland's perceived place in the national pecking order.

"Our goals were set high," Doron said. "I remember my first media day here, and [the media] were like, 'What are your goals?' and I said a national championship and an ACC championship. Maybe it was a little bit naïve since I had never picked up a college basketball, but I never thought we were going to lose."

There was nothing resembling an ACC or national championship in the 2003-04 season, but Doron's fearless competitiveness took hold with her teammates. In her first Maryland game, she tied a NCAA record by making 23 free throws in a 79-64 win against Coppin State. The Terps, playing a schedule conducive to a fast start, won six of their first seven games. There was still work to do in terms of getting everyone to buy into Frese's system, but the arrival of Doron, France and Noirez brought a permanent shift in the team's attitude.

After the fast start, the Terps, still undermanned by ACC standards, battled through conference play, struggling with the league's elite but generally beating teams of equal or lesser talent, which put them squarely on the NCAA Tournament bubble. Maryland entered its final regular-season game at Clemson with an ACC record of 7-8 and knowing that eight wins in conference play usually brought an NCAA bid. The Tigers also were 7-8 in league play, so in the minds of the Maryland coaching staff it was an elimination game. The winner wasn't guaranteed anything, but the loser definitely wasn't going anywhere but the Women's National Invitation Tournament.

Led by Doron and France, the Terps invaded Littlejohn Coliseum and posted an 80-69 victory. After winning its quarterfinal ACC Tournament game against Florida State and losing to Duke in the semifinals, Maryland awaited Selection Sunday. A .500 record in ACC play was generally good enough to earn a tournament bid, but the Terps were 17-12 entering the tournament and didn't have a signature non-conference victory. Frese and her team watched the selection show in Heritage Hall at Comcast Center and were equal parts relieved and thrilled to see their name called as a No. 12 seed, meaning they were one of the final at-large teams in the field.

Not content with merely being in the tournament, the Terps upset fifth-seeded Miami 86-85 in the first round of the West Region before falling to LSU 76-61. Picked to finish eighth in the league, Maryland finished third while ending 18-13 overall. Doron, who arrived on campus saying she didn't expect to lose, averaged 13.5 points and 3.7 rebounds en route to earning third-team All-ACC honors, the first freshman in school history to earn all-conference honors. France was nearly her equal, averaging 11.7 points and 6.0 rebounds.

As gratifying as the on-court turnaround was, it was Frese's success on the recruiting trail that hinted of what was to come. Pursuing the biggest names in an extraordinarily talented class, Frese signed Crystal Langhorne, Laura Harper, Jade Perry and Newman to give Maryland the nation's second-best class.

With this influx of talent, the Terps entered the 2004-05 season expecting to take a significant step forward. Langhorne, Harper and Perry provided the talent, size and athleticism that had been missing up front, and Newman supplied quality depth in a talented backcourt. Maryland started the year ranked 24th nationally and won 10 of its first 11 games, falling only to second-ranked LSU, 64-51, in Boulder, Colo.

But on Dec. 27, 2004, the Terps suffered a crippling blow. Harper was running along the Comcast Center baseline with nobody around when she crumpled. Floyd told Frese she had heard something pop, and a hush fell over the scene except for Harper's cries.

Trainer Matt Charvat carted Harper back to the training room as soon as they could get her up, and Frese restarted practice. Soon, though, she turned matters over to her assistants and went to check on Harper. She arrived in the training room to find the nearly hysterical Harper talking to her mother and brother on the telephone. Charvat delivered the bad news: Every test indicated a complete rupture of the Achilles tendon, a diagnosis confirmed by an MRI a short time later.

Frese worked to get Harper calmed down, assuring her that teammates and coaches would be by her side. For an 18-year-old athlete who had never suffered a serious injury, the realization was shocking.

"Basketball is almost everything to me," Harper said. "It's why I came to school, it's what makes school possible. It's what I live for."

Just that quickly, Harper's season ended. Team surgeon Craig Bennett repaired the severed tendon, and Harper started a long rehabilitation process. The physical part of rehabilitation is taxing, but it's also very straightforward. Athletes are used to pushing their bodies to get bigger, faster and stronger, so the agonizing process is an extension of what they do on a daily basis.

Frese's biggest concern was Harper's mental recovery. When an athlete is injured and can't contribute, there is a tendency to separate from the team — something Frese wanted to prevent. The freshman year is the most difficult for any college student, and she didn't want Harper to fall into a funk while being away from home and her teammates. The night she suffered the injury, teammates stayed with Harper in her dorm room, and she traveled with the team for the rest of the season, with the exception of one trip.

"I wouldn't have been able to do it without my teammates and coaches," Harper said. "They kept me on board. They made me feel like part [of the team], and that really made it better. I was very happy to be able to travel with the team, because I'm a very emotional person. I felt like I was a piece of this team, so I wanted to be there."

That made Harper feel better, but there were no short-term benefits to her absence from the court. She was averaging 13.2 points and a team-leading 9.8 rebounds and, with three double-doubles, performed even better than anticipated.

With the start of ACC play just days away, Frese, who had never dealt with such a severe injury to a key player, felt sick to her stomach. Her own college career was cut short by foot problems, so Frese knew firsthand the mental and physical pain Harper was enduring. Secondly, no matter how well Langhorne and Perry responded, the loss of Harper lowered her team's ceiling.

For those paying attention, Harper's injury allowed Frese to showcase several of her greatest strengths as a coach. While she was still an exceedingly young coach by any measure, Frese's ability to connect with people and gauge the pulse of her team are critical to her success. Frese could have left Harper at home on road trips. Why spend meal money and buy a plane ticket for someone with no chance to play again that season? Most coaches would have left her behind, but Frese took a longer view. Harper remained close to the team, and Frese earned her respect as someone who cared for her for more than just the 40 minutes of each game.

After Harper's MRI verified the rupture, Frese worried over how to best help her team cope with and overcome the injury. The direction she took spoke volumes about her mindset.

She told the Terps of the severity of Harper's injury but also reminded them they had lost only one game. Instead of focusing on what the team had lost, she emphasized what it had to gain. The injury forced Langhorne to shoulder a heavier load in the post, and it moved Perry into the starting lineup, providing her with invaluable experience that would benefit the 2005-06 team immeasurably.

With Langhorne, who would go onto win ACC Rookie of the Year honors, playing an increasingly prominent role and Doron, who earned first-team all-ACC honors, leading the way, Maryland finished the year 22-10, including a 15-point home win against fifth-ranked North Carolina, and earned a No. 7 seed in the NCAA Tournament. The Terps served as a host for the first two tournament rounds and knocked off Wisconsin-Green Bay 65-55 before falling to Ohio State 75-65.

The 20-win season was Maryland's first since 1993, and the only significant departing player was point guard Anesia Smith. The Terps again excelled in recruiting, this time landing Toliver and Coleman.

The public start of the 2005-06 season came on October 15 with Maryland Madness, a historically midnight celebration on the first day the NCAA permits full team practices. The event is all pomp and circumstance, but the players enjoy a turn in the spotlight before practicing in anonymity for a month. The evening, which is shared with the Maryland men's team, included a rousing individual introduction of each player, a scrimmage and giveaways for the thousands of students who packed the Comcast Center.

With the arena lights out and a spotlight following the players through the hallway entrance onto the court, nobody appreciated the moment more than Harper. A player with almost boundless energy, she was ecstatic to be putting on a uniform again. She danced in the holding area while waiting for her name to be called, then bounded onto the court with the smile of someone returning to a place she loves.

The Elkins Park, Pa., native worked for 10 months to get to the point where she could return to the court. Harper attacked the recovery process as soon as her health allowed. She was forced to keep her left foot and ankle immobilized for 2 1/2 months after the surgery, an extremely delicate time for someone recovering from an Achilles rupture. As the tendon heals, an individual feels better and wants to begin increasing the activity level, which can lead to a second rupture. For Harper, who is always going 100 miles per hour, the period of immobilization was horrible.

After being cleared to begin exercising in March, she did range of motion exercises and worked on agility and strength, trying to make sure her mind, ankle and Achilles were functioning as one. When Harper was told she could do one thing, she asked to do 10.

"She's so excitable and energetic, the biggest thing was holding her back," trainer Charvat said. "Her work ethic is something that makes a trainer happy. She always called to see what she could do. It's unusual to have someone that excited about rehab. People will usually go through a little bit of depression with an injury like this. But Harp never went through that."

Just the opposite, Harper ran afoul of Charvat on several occasions for doing too much. She rehabbed for up to two hours a day, four times per week, and as Harper progressed, she began lobbying the careful Charvat and Frese to do more. Recovery from a ruptured Achilles tendon typically takes between eight and 10 months, but exercising an abundance of caution, the Terps' brain trust pushed Harper toward the 10-month mark.

She started jogging lightly in July, and in August began working in a new SwimEx machine the athletic department acquired that allowed her to run under water without forcing the injured leg to bear weight. When the team started individual workouts, she was allowed to participate, primarily to begin polishing her footwork, but even then caution was the operative word. Harper wasn't cleared to begin running full court 5-on-5 until Maryland Madness, and there were periods of intense frustration when she wanted to push the pace.

"I was ahead of schedule," she said of rehab. "It was frustrating not understanding the big picture and what the coaches and doctor saw for me. The season ended in April, and I was trying to come back in July."

Much of that frustration was a thing of the past as she skipped onto the Comcast Center floor with her mother watching from the stands. Later, the two women would share a good cry.

While Harper couldn't beg her way onto the court in the summer of 2005, several of her teammates couldn't stay off it. Langhorne, Coleman and Doron were preparing for the season by playing in Tunisia, Czech Republic, Israel and other distant locales as part of their participation in international competition.

Langhorne and Coleman, a rising freshman, tried out for and made the Under-19 United States National Team coached by Duke coach Gail Goestenkors. The team played around the globe, winning the FIBA U19 World Championship in Tunis, Tunisia, capturing the gold medal at the 2005 International Sports Festival in San Diego and splitting a pair of games against Hungary in Budapest. In addition to becoming more

familiar with each other, Langhorne and Coleman grew from the experiences in different ways.

A native of Willingboro, N.J., Langhorne is supremely talented and
unfailingly polite. She averaged 17.2 points and 10.6 rebounds and shot
59.2 percent from the field as a freshman, but Frese wanted her to
become one of the team's leaders. The international experience didn't
turn Langhorne into a kind of leader who grabs a team by the throat and
demands performance, but it was a great experience for a young player
growing into her role.

As for her play, she averaged 16.6 points and 6.4 rebounds and was
named Most Valuable Player on a squad that included North Carolina's
Erlana Larkins, Tennessee's Nicky Anosike and Oklahoma's Courtney
Paris. Langhorne was a tri-captain and MVP of the U19 World
Championships, averaging 16.6 points and 6.4 rebounds

For Coleman, the international experience played a huge role in
preparing her for life as a college athlete. The 6-foot-1 swing player is a
treasured commodity in women's basketball: someone with broad shoulders, long arms and the ability to play in the post or on the perimeter.

Because of her enormous physical gifts, Coleman was rarely pushed
in high school, despite playing for St. John's in the competitive
Washington Catholic Athletic Conference. She was able to coast through
games on the defensive end, but that wasn't the case in the U19 practices
nor would it be so at Maryland. Goestenkors, who practiced the team
twice a day, rode Coleman about her work habits and defense. Coleman
didn't always appreciate the attention, but it helped make her transition
in October easier. As Frese joked, "I can thank Gail for breaking her in
for what a Division I practice was like." In her second year with the U19
team, Coleman averaged 8.8 points and 4.4 rebounds, but her education
went beyond the stat sheet.

In accordance with her background, Doron enjoyed an extraordinarily diverse summer of 2005, playing for two national teams. Born in
Ramat-Aviv, Israel, Doron played for Israeli and American national
teams, leading both to championships and making some history along
the way. She led Israel to the 2005 Division B European Championship
in Brno, Czech Republic, averaging a tournament high 24.7 points and
earning MVP honors. The triumph was the first international title for an
Israeli women's team.

Afterward, Doron returned to the land of her birth as a member of
the American team at the Maccabi Games. She proceeded to lead the
U.S. team to a 5-0 record and collected MVP honors for the second time.
Doron was called upon to lead both teams, something Frese would

require of her months later.

Toliver's summer unfolded far differently than those experienced by her traveling teammates. She tried out for the U19 National Team, making it to the last round of cuts before being released. Not used to rejection, Toliver was bitterly disappointed, but it allowed her to attend two sessions of summer school in College Park.

In an era when self-promotion is sometimes valued as much as skill, Toliver goes about her business quietly. Whether she is draining three-pointers or turning the ball over at a pace that prematurely ages Frese, her face remains placid. On the court, where she rarely struggles, that quality serves her well. Off the court, she exudes an "everything is good" vibe as well, no matter how turbulent things may become.

As it is for many new college students, the initial adjustment was difficult for Toliver as she learned the nuances of life as a college student and basketball player. Unlike high school, where teachers often operate around a student's schedule, life on campus dictates students learn to work within the parameters established by professors. Toliver struggled with her organizational skills, and the poker face that serves her well on the court wasn't helpful in dealing with academic issues. She didn't reach out for help when it was available and didn't generally ask questions when she had them, making the summer sessions a learning experience for her and the Maryland staff.

Frese, wary of homesickness and how athletes will adjust to being on their own for the first time, is always in close contact with her freshmen, but quickly learned Toliver's cool exterior and "everything is OK" look could belie problems. The Terps' work to get Toliver to be more vocal on the court was just beginning, and the same was true of her efforts in the classroom.

The summer wasn't all about struggling for Toliver. Lifting weights in a structured system for the first time, she packed on 22 pounds of muscle, strengthening her 5-7 frame for the rigors of ACC play.

While their teammates were trotting the globe, rehabbing and adjusting to life on campus, Perry and Newman enjoyed an old-fashioned summer. There was nothing fancy about their training regimens; they just worked. Both had solid freshmen seasons but saw the potential for growth. Perry is undersized for a post player, generously listed at 6-1, but has tremendous physical strength and provides a nice counterbalance to the length and athleticism of Harper and Langhorne.

In high school, Perry was a dominant offensive player, overpowering the small-school competition in her home state of Kentucky. In college, her role changed. The Terps post players could score so Perry focused the majority of her efforts on defense, setting screens and doing the dirty work that can help make a good team great. She worked with Maryland strength and conditioning coach Corliss Fingers to lose weight and improve her foot speed, and the results were readily apparent.

Newman did everything the coaching staff asked of her. She got in the best shape of her life and, realizing there would be a fight for playing time, dedicated herself to improving her defense. Newman correctly figured that on a team full of players capable of scoring, being able to play defense would guarantee her minutes.

The eighth player the Terps were hoping to have as a significant part of their rotation was France. After an excellent freshman campaign, she battled knee tendinitis throughout her sophomore season. France played in all 32 games, starting 31, but her numbers dropped to 11 points and 4.8 rpg — and she was clearly limited. With a summer of rest and rehabilitation, the Terps hoped the 2003 Gatorade Player of the Year in Maryland would return at full strength.

Colleges across the country fund coach's shows, 30-minute programs that typically highlight the team's previous week and include a conversation with the head coach. The shows are designed, in theory, to bring exposure to the team and university and aid recruiting. In reality, the shows have archaic formats, lack creativity and are insufferably boring as coaches talk over snippets of game highlights. When Frese took over at Maryland, she changed nearly all facets of the program, including the coach's show. She didn't want a "Brenda Frese" show. She wanted something showcasing the team in a creative and watchable way.

With Yow's support, Frese contracted with Jess Atkinson, a former

Terps kicker and TV sports anchor, to produce "Under The Shell," a cutting-edge documentary to chronicle Maryland's season. Atkinson and his technicians have complete access to the program. From practice to locker room, the cameras roll, and the result is a compelling show with exceedingly high production values. The show has the residual benefit of preparing players for the presence of cameras.

"Under The Shell" also turned out to be a life-changing venture for Frese. The show's primary videographer and editor during her third season was Mark Thomas, a veteran of the area sports scene who also was contracted by the United States Soccer Federation to produce a documentary on the U.S. National Men's Soccer Team. Thomas traveled with the Terps and developed an immediate bond with Frese.

Both had blond hair, a taste for traveling and, as it turned out, each other. Their relationship blossomed quickly, and they found themselves in love. Thomas, having worked in sports media for years, understood the demands on Frese's time. Between travel, recruiting and the accompanying stress, being the spouse of a coach isn't always easy, but Thomas was an ideal mate. On Aug. 20, 2005, the couple married. Both personally and professionally, her life was better than it had ever been. She got one ring from Thomas, and as the basketball season dawned, she was hoping to collect a second one.

After all the passports were stamped, and everyone returned to campus, Frese held the first team meeting on Sept. 1, 2005. She didn't write national championship, Final Four or ACC championship on the chalkboard as goals. The expectation Frese has for her teams is they work hard and improve. She didn't want to define success for her team in September by what it might do the following March, but she made one thing clear: This was a team with understandably different expectations than her previous three Maryland squads.

"This is a national program now," she told her team. "We've set a very high standard for ourselves, higher than we've ever set here before. We have a chance to do some things that have never been done in the history of the program, but you have to hold yourself accountable and hold each other accountable. If we do that, we will be able to accomplish anything."

Accountability became the fall buzzword for the Terps — it was even stitched on their practice shorts — and it didn't take long for Frese to hold the team accountable for the individual's mistakes.

Angel Ross, one of only two seniors, along with Charmaine Carr, broke her kneecap in the spring, a devastating injury that required surgery and dealt a crushing blow to any chance she had of earning a spot in the rotation. Ross started 23 of 28 games as a freshman, averaging 6 points and 5 rebounds per game, but she became a victim of Frese's success on the recruiting trail and saw her playing time diminish. Because of the severity of the injury, which required surgery and complete immobilization of the leg for a period of time, Ross was still doing rehab work in the fall, and she missed a scheduled appointment.

Frese told the team to be in the Comcast Center the next morning at 6 — they were all going to run. Admittedly not a morning person, Frese wasn't happy to be there, and neither was anyone else. To further compound matters, Ross, still battling the knee injury, couldn't run. She sat at mid-court and watched while her teammates, howling about their fate and Ross' role in it, were forced to run.

The message was sent, but the Terps weren't finished with their early-morning jaunts. Walz passed Coleman and Toliver heading across campus on Coleman's scooter — in a classic freshman mistake, they waved to him — and he immediately realized they were late to class. Frese ordered the team in for another early-morning run and delivered a stern message.

"If you miss a class or are late to class, it's unacceptable," she told her team. "We've got student-athletes representing women's basketball walking into class 10-15 minutes late. I don't care if you are two minutes late, that's unacceptable. You should be there ahead of time. That's unacceptable behavior, and it won't be tolerated."

Maryland didn't have another early-morning run the rest of the season.

Shortly after the Sept. 1 meeting, the Terps started individual workouts and the staff, for the third consecutive year, realized the team was much more talented and skilled than its predecessor. Once full-squad practice began, Maryland was erratic in the opening weeks, flashing the brilliance it would display the following March on good days and staging a comedy of errors during bad practices. Toliver, as all freshmen point guards do, struggled to learn the offense, but she didn't have the luxury of learning with the second unit. When Toliver signed her national letter of intent, she inherited control of the Maryland offense. Whether she was good, bad or indifferent, there wasn't a backup plan.

When she struggled, the entire offense sagged, prompting Joanna Bernabei to say, "There were days I would go home and tell my husband, we could be unbelievable this year, and there were days I would go home and say we might not win half our conference games."

Though the offense sputtered on occasion, Frese knew she had a talented core returning and had seen enough of Toliver and Coleman to know scoring wouldn't be a problem. While there was considerable time and effort put into Toliver's development, the thrust of Maryland's preseason efforts revolved around defense and rebounding.

Maryland could allow 75 or 80 points and win on most nights. If the team was to take the next step, it would have to be able to stop the most talented teams on the schedule and deny them second-chance opportunities. The players set a season-long goal of not allowing opponents to score more than 70 points, reasoning they would always score at least that many. The early results were mixed. Playing against a scout team that consisted of four male players, the Terps often floundered, getting beat off the dribble and struggling on the boards. They didn't lose every scrimmage, but they lost more often than Frese liked to see.

With strong perimeter play throughout the ACC, the Terps placed particular emphasis on stopping dribble penetration and defending off the ball. For many observers, defense is about effort. The thinking goes if a player wants to play good defense, he or she should be able to do so through willpower alone. There is some truth to that because nobody has ever played good defense without an abundance of effort, but it also oversimplifies a complex aspect of the game.

Learning to defend off the ball or knowing when, how and from what position to double-team comes with experience and a feel for the game that effort alone can't provide. Though there were days when the coaches wondered if and when the work the team was putting in would take hold on a consistent basis, they were generally encouraged.

Frese talked to her team about the changing expectations of the program in their first team meeting, and most of what she saw in the first month of practice led her to believe her team was capable, at the very least, of reaching heights not seen in College Park in 15 years.

Chapter 3

A Young Pup Bites

T here is a Southern adage that Maryland director of athletics Debbie Yow subscribes to: If a dog is going to bite you, it will bite you as a pup. When Yow went in search of a new women's basketball coach, there wasn't a pup in the game biting more people than Frese (then Brenda Oldfield). Just 31, she already had three years of head coaching experience while returning floundering programs at Ball State and Minnesota to prominence.

Frese rescued Minnesota's program from turmoil and turned the Golden Gophers into a success on and off the court, solidifying her reputation as one of the game's rising stars. She also caught the eye of Yow, who built Kentucky, Florida and Oral Roberts into top 20 programs as a coach before moving into athletic administration. The more Yow learned about Frese, the more she liked her, and when Weller retired in early March 2002, the young Minnesota coach sat atop Maryland's wish list.

When the Golden Gophers completed their magical 2002 season with a 72-69 NCAA Tournament second-round loss to North Carolina in Chapel Hill on March 18, the Terps began their pursuit in earnest. Frese knew little about Maryland. She had spent her life in the Midwest, with the exception of her college years in Arizona. Her only experience with the College Park area was an annual trip to scout the U.S. Junior Nationals and the time she spent sitting in traffic. Frese was one of the game's hottest names and Yow was her most ardent pursuer. As the Terrapins men's team was making its NCAA Tournament title run, Yow and the search committee were actively engaged with Frese.

Any uncertainty felt by Frese for Maryland ended when arriving for an interview after Minnesota's season ended. What she found on the interview couldn't have been further from the feeling of sitting in snarled suburban Washington, D.C. Beltway traffic. With the hoopla surrounding the men's tournament in full bloom, Yow flew Frese in for a one-day interview that ended with both parties more impressed than either had imagined.

"Listening to Debbie Yow on the phone, she convinced me to come on a visit, and once I got there, I was blown away," Frese said. "They took me to the top of Comcast Center, and I knew then, if they offered me this job, I was going to take it. I could just feel and see the vision [Yow had for the program]."

From Yow's perspective, she saw the passion, intelligence and hunger in a coach that could take Maryland to the top. Yow and Frese each left the interview believing to have found what she was looking for. Yow wanted the Maryland women's team to return to prominence; Frese was looking for a job with the resources to contend for a national title.

Frese was soon named Associated Press Coach of the Year, a wonderful personal award but an unwanted complication from Maryland's perspective. She was a hot name. Ohio State and Florida inquired about her availability after the AP honor and Frese went through a cursory interview with the Buckeyes in San Antonio at the women's Final Four. There was little doubt over her choice, however.

Oddly silent during Maryland's courtship of Frese was Minnesota, which knew the terms of the contract signed 10 months earlier. She was the youngest head coach in the Big Ten and among the lowest-paid. After Frese led Minnesota to a 14-game improvement in her one season, the school's administration had to know she would be a hot commodity. It also knew the contract, almost inexplicably, didn't have a buyout clause to discourage other schools from pursuing her. Frese didn't object to a buyout clause being placed in her contract, Minnesota just failed to include it.

The Gophers were under no obligation to renegotiate Frese's contract, but were aware of the potential consequences. Coaches are often hired away with time remaining on a contract.

By March 29, Frese was in San Antonio for the women's Final Four, and Yow was in Atlanta for the men's event, but the two sides had nearly come to terms.

While mulling Maryland's offer, Frese finally received a call from Minnesota President Mark Yudof, who congratulated her on being named coach of the year. Yudof also acknowledged Maryland's interest and asked when Frese planned to sit down and talk with the Golden Gophers about her contract. Frese said she didn't know. No one at Minnesota had approached her about the contract, and Frese was getting very close to making a decision on Maryland's offer.

Yudof called an emergency meeting on March 31, and Frese hopped the next flight back to Minneapolis. Ultimately, the Gophers offered her more money than Maryland, which was significant because the cost of living in College Park is substantially higher, but offered only minimal raises for her staff, making the decision an easy one. Frese wanted to win at the highest level and felt Maryland offered the best chance. Considering Comcast Center, the vision she shared with Yow, and nagging behind-the-scenes problems in Minnesota, the decision wasn't difficult. On April 1, 2002, Frese agreed to become the third head coach in the history of Maryland women's basketball.

If the decision to accept the Maryland job wasn't hard, its aftermath was. Though Frese accepted the job on April 1, her introductory press conference wasn't scheduled until two days later. She was going to use the day between to tell her players at Minnesota. But 48 hours is a long time to keep a secret in Washington, and word of her hiring leaked to the press. Watching the Maryland men's team defeat Indiana for the national title on TV, Frese saw her hiring scroll across the bottom of the screen. Her chin nearly hit the floor. Frese was stunned, and so were her players.

Frese and her staff, all of whom were going with her to Maryland, met with the Minnesota team at 8 the next morning in an off-campus apartment complex. The meeting ran the gamut of emotions. The room pulsed with anger, sorrow and bewilderment as Frese attempted to explain a decision that was impossible for her players to understand. It was a move that was in her professional best interest, but the relationship between Frese and the Gophers players was very personal. Just a year earlier, Minnesota had been adrift at the end of Littlejohn's tenure, and Frese helped the players restore pride to the program. Now many of those players would be forced to deal with their third coach in as many years. The way the Minnesota players learned of her departure was one of Frese's true regrets.

"It was horrible," Frese said of the meeting. "My number one concern is for the players, and they didn't deserve to find out that way."

A media darling during her season in Minneapolis, Frese, who is very accessible to the press, was savaged for her decision. Everything from the way she dressed to her maturity was called into question by the jilted Gophers. Neither fans nor the media bothered to consider Minnesota had done the same thing Ball State did when hiring Frese. For that matter, the Golden Gophers also lured head men's coach Don Munson away from Gonzaga. Frese didn't do anything differently than millions of other people each year, particularly young ones. Frese accepted what she thought was a better job.

Frese's appointment in College Park continued her dramatic rise through the coaching ranks. A decade earlier, dealing with the aftermath of nearly crippling foot problems, Frese was still on scholarship at Arizona but was a member of the team in name only. The two years she battled problems with her feet gave Frese plenty of time to think about her future. If she couldn't play basketball, she wanted to coach it. Rather than spend her time in the Arizona program, where her experience would have been limited primarily to clerical work, she went to nearby Pima Community College. As the only assistant coach at Pima, Frese took on a lot of responsibility. Head coach Susie Polido let her dabble in all aspects of coaching, and Frese was immediately drawn in. Frese, still a 22-year-old college student, was handling practices, making halftime speeches and driving school vans. She was about as far from a Division I head coaching job as one could possibly be, but it was an outlet for her competitive juices.

Frese was slated to graduate from Arizona in 1993, and she wanted to coach at the Division I level. She asked Arizona coach Joan Bonvicini for assistance in finding a job, but in typical Frese fashion didn't leave her fate to someone else.

Her younger sister, Stacy, a highly regarded high school player at the time, was being recruited by numerous schools. Brenda, hoping to take advantage of her sister's recruitment, sent resumes to every school contacting Stacy. With Stacy's name generating little interest, Brenda took a more aggressive approach. Accompanied by her boyfriend at the time, she piled into her red Beretta — a car her father bought her when she accepted the scholarship to Arizona — and drove from Tucson to Atlanta, site of the 1993 women's Final Four.

It took more than 24 hours to travel 1,700-plus miles, but Frese is nothing if not determined. Arriving in Atlanta, she began looking for familiar faces. Frese hoped her own face was still familiar to coaches she had competed against and seen while working at Mike Flynn's Blue Star Camps during the summer. Working the people she knew, Frese learned Kent State was looking for a graduate assistant. She had two questions: Who and where was the coach?

Bob Lindsay was the Kent State coach, and Frese found him at a Final Four party. She introduced herself and chatted with the Golden Flashes' boss for 15 minutes. She sent him a resume upon returning to Tucson and a month later was offered the job. It was Frese's only offer.

Her arrival in Kent, Ohio, provided her with a dose of financial reality. Between the money she received from her scholarship stipend and her work at Pima, Frese had been flush by the standards of a college student, pulling in $1,000 a month. When she got to Kent State, she received $500 per month to cover all of her expenses, forcing her to wait tables in the spring and summer to generate additional funds. She was also faced with a bit of coaching reality: She wasn't going to be running practices and delivering speeches as a graduate assistant. Her primary responsibility was film exchange and breaking tape down once it arrived.

Charged with obtaining film on upcoming opponents, Frese did what she thought was logical: She called the opposition and asked them to send tapes of recent games. Unfortunately, that isn't how it works. Coaches don't send game tapes to future opponents. When Frese called and asked for tape, the person on the other end of the line usually had a "do you know what the hell you are doing" tone in his or her voice until someone was kind enough to tell her how film exchange was handled. Schools obtain tape for upcoming games by contacting an opponent of its opponents. The revelation left Frese, in her words, feeling like a "moron." But as she always seems to do, Frese learned from her mistake and was rewarded. A full-time assistant left Lindsay's staff after the 1993-94 season, and Frese was rewarded with the full-time position.

The promotion was beneficial both personally and professionally. The job allowed Frese to start recruiting, where she honed her skills. She was a natural on the road. Easy to engage in conversation and quick-witted, Frese built up a network of contacts, and working for Lindsay challenged her. He was an analytical coach who would send Frese to scout a game but not tell her exactly who she was watching. It was unconventional and very stressful, but it forced Frese to watch everybody on the floor. Lindsay didn't want his assistants to be narrowly focused when scouting, a valuable lesson at the mid-major level.

When Frese moved up the pecking order, Lindsay hired another young coach, Erica Floyd, with whom Frese struck an immediate and lasting friendship.

Even with just one year as a full-time assistant, Frese stood out. She attracted the attention of Iowa State coach Bill Fennelly, who asked Lindsay for permission to interview her and hired her shortly thereafter. Just three years after driving kids to games in vans at Pima CC, Frese was on staff at Iowa State. For the first time it dawned on Frese that she was on a fast track, and she was initially concerned about doing a credible job at the high-major level. Despite occasionally feeling overwhelmed, Frese worked and learned. Frese was like a sponge during her four years in Ames. She absorbed everything Fennelly did from halftime speeches to home visits. She proved to be a quick study. By her third year, Frese earned Fennelly's complete trust in player evaluation. She also developed her passion for recruiting during her time in Ames — and suffered a loss Frese still calls her most devastating.

Frese threw her heart into the recruiting of Mary Berdo, an in-state star. She believed Berdo was going to be a Cyclone until the moment the player committed to Iowa instead. "I had never invested that much time in a kid," Frese recalled. "I remember the other assistant saying, 'How could you be that upset?' I was crushed."

The disappointment Frese felt in losing Berdo was instructive, because she is driven by passion more than anything else. Fortunately for her mental health, the triumphs outnumbered the setbacks, and Iowa State enjoyed unprecedented success during her tenure.

There was another Frese who played an instrumental role in Iowa State's success. Stacy, who committed to Iowa out of high school, transferred to Iowa State, where she played under the watchful eye of her sister. A three-time all-Big 12 selection, Stacy was the Cyclones' point guard, and home games were like a Frese family reunion. In Brenda's final two seasons in Ames, Iowa State went 50-16 and advanced to the Elite Eight in 1999, knocking off Connecticut along the way.

Frese was ready to take the next step, assuming she could convince an athletic director to hire a 29-year-old head coach. She got the break she was looking for when Ball State called. With a record of 66-169 in the nine years before Frese's arrival, Ball State wasn't a cradle of coaches, but Frese was delighted to have the opportunity. After flying in the night before, she went through an exhausting 12-hour interview, and seemingly talked to everyone on campus. Whatever Frese said worked, because she got the head coaching job she coveted.

The responsibility was immense. Frese went from making suggestions to making decisions, and the challenge was daunting. "The first month was mind-boggling. I remember saying to myself, 'I don't know if I'm set up or good enough to do this job,' " she said. "Nobody tells you how to be a head coach. It tests your character and integrity. You have to make decisions in a hurry, and it has to be within your value system. I didn't have to make those decisions as an assistant."

Frese reached out to her new team, trying to establish relationships with the players and, to some degree, re-recruit them. She demanded more of her players than they were accustomed to giving, and none tested her more than freshman Tamara Bowie, who was as talented as she was strong willed. It seemed every time Frese made a decision, Bowie questioned it, but even as a first-year coach, Frese was able to reach her players on a personal level while demanding excellence on the court.

"At the beginning, I guess you could say it was a love-hate thing. I loved the fact she made me work hard, and at the same time I hated her for it," Bowie said with a laugh. "I gave her a lot of problems in the beginning. I thought everything was stupid, but I started believing in everything she put on the table."

Ball State improved quicker than anyone could have imagined. The Cardinals hadn't had a winning season since 1990, but Frese quickly let everyone know things were going to change in Muncie, Ind. On Nov. 20, 1999, she led her Ball State team onto the court for the first time, ironically at Minnesota in the Golden Gophers' season-opening tournament. Ball State and its new coach were brought in to be sacrificial lambs for Minnesota, but a young pup bit her first foe that evening. In a game that surely resonated when Minnesota was looking for a new coach two years later, the Cardinals stunned the Gophers 79-70. Frese and her players were jubilant, but she had to battle opening game jitters. Ball State scored late in the game, a timeout was called and Frese was full of excitement. Unfortunately, in this case, it was misdirected.

"I'm meeting with my assistants, and we are going back out on defense," Frese recalled with a laugh. "I tell the team to start getting in a press breaker [offense]. I was out of it. I remember diagramming it up, and [the players] were like, 'Coach, we are on defense.' I was like, 'Get out there and get a stop.' "

Frese laughs at the memory, but Ball State provided her with tremendous experience. She learned to handle a staff, the media, disciplinary problems and everything else that accompanies being a head coach. Just as she grew, so did her team. After finishing 16-13 in her first season, Ball State went 19-9 in 2000-01. Her revival of the previously moribund program turned heads throughout the Midwest, and Minnesota came calling after the season.

Telling the players at Ball State she was leaving was difficult, but at least one of them understood. Frese discussed her dream of winning a national championship with Bowie and encouraged the player to aspire to great heights as well. Bowie knew Frese wouldn't be at Ball State long regardless of her youth.

"I had my basketball dream at the time," Bowie said. "Before she left, she said, 'Don't let this affect you. Keep working hard to do the things to make you better.' I didn't know what I had in front of me until she was gone. She helped me grow as a student-athlete and a person."

Bowie and Frese continued to keep in touch, and when Bowie was one of the Washington Mystics final cuts in 2003, she joined Frese's staff at Maryland as assistant director of basketball operations.

When Frese was offered the Minnesota job, the program was reeling from the tumult of Littlejohn's tenure, but opportunities to coach in the Big Ten are limited. There was some thought the job wasn't a good one because of the NCAA problems and the program's traditional lack of success, but Frese's dreams were big. She wanted to win a national championship, and it wasn't going to happen at Ball State.

The Gophers were a disaster the year before Frese arrived, losing their last 11 games and 17 of 18 overall, and rarely being competitive. Frese and her staff were unsure what to expect. After watching film and going through individual workouts, they were pleasantly surprised. Minnesota's 8-20 record might have been an embarrassment, but their talent level wasn't. With future All-Americans Lindsay Whalen and Janel McCarville on the roster, the Gophers were waiting for the right coach to awaken them.

Minnesota won 12 of its first 14 games, and a team that was 1-15 in Big Ten play the year before went 11-5 against league opponents. The Gophers also received a literal break that turned into a boon for the program. Minnesota opened the year playing in the Sports Pavilion, a facility seating fewer than 6,000. Frese wanted to outgrow the building and play in Williams Arena, the university's larger men's facility. With Minnesota's momentum building coming off an 83-75 win against No. 13 Purdue, the team was preparing to leave for a trip to Wisconsin when a water pipe exploded and water flooded the floor, rendering it unplayable for the rest of the season. The Gophers went on the road, upset the fifth-ranked Badgers 92-85 and the team's popularity soared.

Minnesota had 11,389 fans packed into Williams Arena for its next home game, a 75-60 win against Indiana, and 12,142 came for the regular-season finale.

Frese's rise through the coaching ranks was quick, but her credentials were impeccable. She had won in places many considered hopeless before her arrival. There was nothing beyond the strength of Frese's will to suggest that Ball State's and Minnesota's fortunes were getting ready to change.

At Maryland, a school with historical success and a brand-new building on the way, the long-term prospects seemed boundless to Frese. Like any athletic director, Yow was ecstatic to land her top candidate and the enormously confident Frese would make Maryland one of the nation's elite teams.

Chapter 4

Almost Paradise

A season with great ambition and hope began about as far from the bright lights of the Final Four as possible. Frese and her 14th-ranked Terps boarded a Southwest Airlines flight on Nov. 17 and flew into Albany, N.Y., for a game the following day against Siena.

Unlike the men's game, where power conference teams rarely play away from home, the women are much more likely to go on the road against teams from smaller conferences. Maryland's tangle with Siena, a small liberal arts school rooted in Franciscan and Catholic traditions, was a prime example. A member of the lightly regarded Metro Atlantic Athletic Conference, the Saints didn't have a particularly strong team, much less one capable of knocking off the Terps. The women's game typically doesn't generate enough revenue for home games to justify paying large sums of money to overmatched teams to visit. Instead, the Terps offer a return date on the road.

What Siena, located in Loudonville, N.Y., lacked in talent, it tried to compensate for with enthusiasm. Against the Terps, the highest-ranked team ever to play at Siena, the Saints packed a record 3,780 fans into the Alumni Recreation Center. If the Siena players were delighted to see the large crowd, so was Maryland. Sure the fans came for the college's celebration of 35 years of women's college basketball, but they also were there to see the highly regarded Terps, an exciting prospect for a young team.

Once the whistle blew, the crowd's energy did the Saints little good. Less than 10 minutes in, the Terps held a 16-point lead and eventually took a 59-31 advantage into the half. The only drama involved an individual exchange that allowed Frese to turn a blowout into a teaching situation. With 16 seconds left in the half, Siena's Lauren Surber drained a three-pointer in Toliver's face, giving the sellout crowd a rare opportunity to cheer. Playing with the moxie that came to define her game and season, Toliver quickly brought the ball back downcourt and made a three-pointer with six seconds remaining, silencing the crowd literally and figuratively. As time expired, Toliver brought her index finger to her lips and shushed the crowd — a move that didn't win Frese's approval, particularly against an overmatched opponent.

Maryland had six players score in double figures, led by Doron's 23, and cruised to a 107-66 victory. Every player except Ross, still out with the knee injury, played at least 15 minutes as Maryland shot 65 percent from the floor and 58 percent from three-point range. The Saints weren't great, but the Terps seized control from the outset. Though Frese was angry at Toliver's gesture to the crowd — seeing no reason to incite or taunt fans in an opposing gym — she waited until the Terps were flying out the following day to address the situation. With the emotions of the game subsided, Frese talked with her rookie point guard about the image she wanted her to project both personally and as a representative of the team and school.

Toliver didn't make the same mistake again, and the incident revealed a side of Toliver the Terps would see throughout the season. She never backed down from a challenge. It didn't matter if the Terps were playing Siena or North Carolina. If an opponent went at Toliver, she was going to respond.

Two days after the Siena game, Maryland blasted Xavier 93-68 in its home opener. The Terps used a 19-0 first half run to take control, and the Musketeers were never in the game. The team again was led in scoring by Doron, who scored 23 points.

———

Two games into the season, Doron, who led the team in scoring each of her first two years, averaging 17.6 points and earning first-team all-ACC honors as a sophomore, appeared to be the leader once more. Doron had scored 20 or more points 13 times as a sophomore and erupted for 37 points in a 92-77 home upset of North Carolina. Two games later, she scored a career-high 39 in a 95-91 overtime loss at Florida State.

Doron had been the team's go-to offensive player practically from the day she set foot on campus, and she remained a potent threat with the ball in her hands. But her junior season was different. The level of

talent surrounding her had increased significantly, and the need for her
to dominate games on the offensive end had lessened. The reduction in
Maryland's reliance on Doron's offense was a reflection on the skill of
her teammates as opposed to any sort of knock on her game, and Doron
understood that separation.

As part of the players being accountable to one another, the development of internal leadership was vital to the team's long-term success.
A player who barks at teammates after mistakes and issues challenges is
typically celebrated as a captain and leader in sports — at least when the
team is winning. The Terps received leadership, but it often came in different forms.

Doron, the team's most experienced player and oldest starter,
helped set the tone with her willingness to accept the fact that she
wouldn't always be the team's No. 1 option. Doron's team-leading 10.5
shots a game were three attempts fewer than during her sophomore season. Fortunately, she was intelligent enough to realize that her willingness to sacrifice shots in some ways increased her importance to the
team.

"Getting everybody involved when you have a team like this with
so many good players [is important]," she said of her new role. "What
better person to prove that's not what we are about [scoring] than me? I
was the leading scorer for two years, but I don't care. I'm here to win a
championship, and people follow my lead. If I was chucking up shots
and not passing the ball, it was going to lead to everyone else doing the
same thing."

Adapting to change had become second nature to Doron, who has
dual Israeli and American citizenship. She shuttled back and forth
between the two countries as a child, never spending more than four
years in one place. Her parents, Yuda and Tamari Doron, were excep-
tional athletes — her mother was a member of the Israeli national vol-
leyball team and her father a tri-athlete — and it didn't take Doron long
to distinguish herself athletically. She excelled in soccer and track, but
basketball was her passion.

She spent her seventh-through-10th grade years in Israel and took
her game as far as possible in her homeland. At one point, Doron played
on five teams, including the national squad, but wanted more. With 11th
grade on the horizon, her parents offered the chance to return to the
United States if she wanted to pursue playing basketball at the highest
level possible — the Women's National Basketball Association. For
Doron, the decision was agonizing. Her family lived in Israel and after
several moves, Doron felt like she had found a home. Ultimately,

Doron's ambition prevailed, and she returned to America.

As a player unknown in the United States, Doron needed to attract the attention of college recruiters quickly. The family went in search of a high-profile prep program and found New York City's Christ the King High School, alma mater of Sue Bird and Chamique Holdsclaw, two of the best women's college basketball players in the history of the game.

It didn't take Doron long to adjust. She was the Gatorade Player of the Year in New York as a junior and senior at Christ the King, but the transition wasn't always easy. She lived in Great Neck, N.Y., with a 45-minute commute to school — on a mini-yellow school bus. For a teenager attending an upscale private school, a yellow school bus isn't the preferred mode of transportation.

"I was like, 'Are they really picking me up in this bus?' " she says now with a laugh. "I didn't mind the ride — it's just when I got there. It was like I had my own private school bus."

Doron left for school at 6 a.m. and often didn't get home until 9 or 10 p.m., but the long hours were rewarded by Maryland's scholarship offer. Sacrificing a couple of shots in pursuit of the title hardly compared with leaving her homeland in the middle of high school.

The trip to Siena and the home opener against Xavier were mere appetizers for the set of games Maryland had been looking forward to all summer: the Paradise Jam in St. Thomas, Virgin Islands. The Terps were going to spend Thanksgiving in one of the Caribbean's most popular vacation destinations for an event that featured eight teams divided into two divisions. Maryland was in the St. Thomas Division along with No. 1-ranked Tennessee, No. 9 Michigan State and Gonzaga.

Before play started, Frese ensured players enjoyed the Caribbean destination. The Maryland delegation boarded a catamaran and headed to sea for a snorkeling trip, a first for several players, and enjoyed the sandy white beaches. The team also attended a dinner hosted by tournament organizers on Paradise Point, a scenic bluff 700 feet above sea level offering a stunning view of St. Thomas Harbor.

The Terps took a gondola ride to the restaurant, and were directed to a group of tables toward the center of the dining area. The view was nice and the food great, but the restaurant's prime seats that offered a more panoramic view of the bay below were reserved for Michigan

State and Tennessee, the event's marquee teams. The Terps took their seats and didn't complain — in the big scheme of things, how could they? However, the incident left a chip on their shoulder that grew through the season. The Terps didn't feel they were getting the respect they deserved.

The weather was perfect and so was the opportunity. The players told anyone who would listen that this year's team was capable of going to the Final Four, and now they had an opportunity to show the talk was more than bluster.

First on the docket was Gonzaga, a small Jesuit school in Spokane, Wash., that rose to prominence in the last decade on the strength of its men's basketball program. The women's team hadn't enjoyed success to the same degree, but it went 28-4 during the 2004-05 season, including a 14-0 record in West Coast Conference play before being upset in the conference tournament and relegated to the Women's National Invitation Tournament for the second consecutive season.

The 2005-06 Zags weren't as strong, but the game was televised on Fox Sports Network, allowing Maryland to make its first statement to the nation. The Terps jumped to a 26-5 lead less than eight minutes in and won 88-50, largely on the strength of a 57-32 rebounding advantage. With Gonzaga dismissed, Maryland turned its attention to Michigan State.

In 2004-05, 39-year-old coach Joanne McCallie led Michigan State to a school-record 33 wins and a spot in the NCAA title game in her fifth season. The Spartans were a rising power in the Big Ten, and the Terps saw the game as an opportunity to boost their national profile.

In her pregame talk, Frese pulled a trump card played repeatedly throughout the season. "How can you not get up for this game?" she asked her team. "This is a game everybody is saying we don't have a chance to win. Everybody is saying we are going 1-2 in this tournament."

For most of the first half, Maryland — which had moved up to 10th in the polls, one spot behind Michigan State — indeed played like a team that didn't have much of a chance. The Terps trailed by as many as 11 points and shot a tepid 29.6 percent from the field. Toliver picked up her second foul just over five minutes into the game, and the offense struggled accordingly. Offensive woes are one thing, but Frese was livid with the lack of toughness her team was showing. "We are backing down from their physicalness," she told the players in an animated voice during the first half. "You step up and play [more physically]."

Maryland responded with more aggressive play, slowly reducing the deficit. After Perry made a layup with four seconds remaining in the half, the team trailed just 33-29. After what could have been a disheartening effort for a young team looking to make a name for itself, the Terps entered the break feeling good. They had played miserably and yet they were just two possessions from the lead. Frese told the team the first four minutes of the second half would be pivotal — they had to let Michigan State know it would be playing a different Maryland team over the final 20 minutes.

Doron's three-pointer with 8:19 remaining gave Maryland the lead for good at 54-51 as a talented young team started to grow up. Led by a defense forcing turnovers and an offense producing layups, the Terps cruised to an impressive 75-61 win.

Maryland hadn't advanced past the second round of the NCAA Tournament in 14 years, and now it was talking of reaching the Final Four. A decisive victory against a team of Michigan State's stature was a big one for the Terps. The victory not only let the rest of the country know of Maryland's rise but instilled a greater sense of confidence within the team.

"We came out with a new focus in the second half," Walz said. "To that point, people were saying we were good but we hadn't beaten a top-ranked team to prove it. The second half was really important for our players."

Frese told her team that if it beat Michigan State she would braid her hair in a style favored on the island and by many American kids. It's hard to imagine Tennessee coach Pat Summitt or some of the game's other prominent coaches with their hair braided, but that's part of what makes Frese successful. She keeps her team loose, at least in part by not taking herself too seriously. A couple of hours and considerably more pain than Frese expected later, she headed back to the hotel with a hairstyle different than any she previously had.

Good times aside, the Terps couldn't have been more serious about the next day's game against Tennessee. After wins on consecutive days in a sweltering gym, the game the Terps had been looking forward to — a showdown with No. 1 ranked Tennessee — loomed. The Maryland traveling party was thinking about going 3-0 in the Paradise Jam, making the Virgin Islands a dream destination on and off the court.

The Terps hadn't faced the Lady Vols on the court since a 95-29 loss in 1994, but since Frese's arrival the two programs had regularly bumped heads on the recruiting trail. Summitt, owner of six national titles and 16 Final Four appearances, had been the face of women's basketball for two decades, making Knoxville, Tenn., the favored destination for many of America's top players. Over the years, Summitt was an integral part of the game's growth in popularity, but there was a drawback. As television coverage of the women's game grew and participation numbers for youth league girls spurted, elite players became much more aware of destinations beyond Knoxville and Storrs, Conn., home of the University of Connecticut, the game's other flagship program.

A younger generation of coaches — led by Frese, Baylor's Kim Mulkey, Louisiana State's Pokey Chatman and others — respected Summitt's accomplishments but felt no need to take a backseat to anyone. Frese assembled Maryland's high-powered roster by encouraging her players to be part of a burgeoning tradition, not one long established. The foundation of Maryland's success rested in the sophomore class — Langhorne, Harper, Newman and Perry — that had been ranked as the second-best in the nation. The nation's top recruiting class in 2005 belonged to Tennessee. It included Candace Parker, Nicky Anosike, Sa'de Wiley-Gatewood and Alexis Hornbuckle — a group UT touted as one of the greatest classes in women's hoops history.

For Maryland's players, games against powers like Tennessee were the reason they elected to go to College Park. Several Terps could have picked Knoxville had they desired, but instead they came to Maryland to help build a program from the ground up. The matchup with the Lady Vols would be a barometer for how much construction the Terps had undergone and how much more was needed.

Frese instructed her players to relax and have fun, cautioning them against being too excited — something she felt had derailed their chance to knock off then-No. 2 LSU the previous season. Maryland took the floor first and Newman, who grew up in Murfreesboro, Tenn., found herself singing "Rocky Top," Tennessee's fight song, when the Lady Vols hit the floor. That was the only concession Maryland made to Tennessee's tradition. Just as Frese attacked the recruiting trail with no fear of confronting Summitt, her players did the same on the court.

Both teams got off to a slow start, something that plagued Maryland all season, before Tennessee opened up a 13-point lead. Just as they had done the day before, the Terps fought back. Powered by Langhorne, the best player on the court that day, Maryland closed within 34-30 at the break, setting the stage for a dramatic second half.

The Terps continued to surge after halftime, taking a 42-41 edge with 16:45 remaining. The lead change was the first of 15 in a second half that prompted Frese to tell Walz that it felt like March. Two of the nation's more talented teams raced up and down the court, scoring points in droves. It was a game of runs, but no lead was larger than an eight-point Maryland cushion that the Lady Vols quickly erased. With Tennessee's defense swarming Langhorne, who finished with 19 points on 8-of-10 shooting, and added 11 rebounds, the game opened up for the perimeter players. Toliver, who had struggled mightily the day before against Michigan State, scored 17 points and drained three three-pointers, and fellow freshman Coleman had 16 points. The talented newcomers were growing up in a hurry. Harper, who felt like a freshman in some ways, banged down low for 13 points and 12 rebounds, helping Maryland control the paint.

A 9-0 Tennessee run erased the Terps' 63-55 lead, and the final six minutes were as tense as it gets for college basketball in November. After the lead changed nine times in a three-minute stretch, Wiley-Gatewood gave Tennessee a lead it wouldn't relinquish at 74-73 with 2:54 left. The Terps, who were able to stay in the game despite 24 turnovers, continued to battle but, perhaps showing their inexperience, committed fatal mistakes down the stretch. With Maryland trailing 76-75 and 11 seconds left, Toliver rebounded a missed Tennessee three-pointer and raced downcourt. A freshman playing in her first tight game, she had a lane to the basket or room for an open shot but opted to try to get the ball to Doron, an upperclassman. The Lady Vols tipped the ball out of bounds with five seconds remaining, and Maryland called a time-out.

The play discussed in the huddle called for Doron to inbound the ball to Harper, who would feed it back to the junior for a potential game-winner. Unfortunately, Doron's pass sailed toward halfcourt, where it was picked off by UT's Sidney Spencer, and Maryland's chance to win evaporated. Tennessee made four free throws in the final two seconds, accounting for the 80-75 final score. The game Maryland dreamed of winning instead ended in nightmarish fashion. Doron was disconsolate in the locker room, her head buried in her hands. Frese correctly told Doron the loss wasn't her fault, but it was of little solace to a player who burned to win as badly as Doron did.

Toliver, who the Maryland staff had urged to be more assertive from the day she set foot on campus, passed up a potential game-winner, deferring to an older player. Blessed with an unselfish team and many players with the ability to score, the one thing Frese wanted her players to do was take a good shot when it was available. Passing up an open shot wasn't a mistake Toliver would make in clutch situations later in the season.

The Terps were disappointed to lose, of course, but the coaching staff saw in its team a fight, a belief, that had been lacking the previous year.

Frese felt her team hadn't always believed it could win against the best teams during her first three years. The same couldn't be said of this team.

"This isn't the end of our season," Langhorne told the team after the game. "We still have ACC [play], the NCAA. We have so much ahead of us, this is just going to make us better."

Frese, looking to build her team's confidence after a difficult loss, took it one step further.

"If that doesn't give you confidence that this is a Final Four team, I don't know what does," she told the players.

As the Terps sat in Cyril E. King Airport in the Virgin Islands, Frese removed the braids from her hair, much to the disappointment of her players, who wanted their coach to bring a little of the island back to College Park. It took five players nearly two hours to help remove the braids. Beyond the pain the braids caused, Frese, who was enjoying the balance her new marriage provided, had off-court matters to tend to. The day after the team returned, Frese and Thomas were closing on a new home.

Chapter 5

"My Stretch of Going Insane"

For Toliver, December was the most difficult month of the season. As the starting point guard on a top 10 team, she bore enormous pressure. With Christie Marrone, a transfer from Virginia Tech, sitting out the year per NCAA transfer requirements, Maryland had no true backup point guard. Toliver was quiet by nature, and the coaching staff was working with her to become more assertive.

The daughter of George Toliver, a longtime NBA official, Kristi had the physical skills and hardwood education to be a star. George started his daughter in the game at a young age, teaching her to shoot with a tennis ball at a three-foot basketball goal from Kmart. George felt shooting with the tennis ball allowed Kristi to learn proper technique because she was able to take a more natural shot rather than forcing a ball that was too large. As Kristi grew, so did the size of the ball. George even traced the outline of her hand on a ball so she could properly position her hands with each shot. In Kristi's case, her father knew best — she grew into a lethal shooter before arriving at College Park.

As important as Toliver's jump shot was to Maryland's success, both short and long term, her ability to handle the ball was critical. In the basement of the family home in Harrisonburg, Va., George turned out the lights and Kristi dribbled in the dark, learning to trust her ability to handle the ball without seeing it. By the time George taped a lane, allowing Kristi to develop a more innate feel for the dimensions of the court, she was rapidly becoming one of the better guards in the nation. She scored a school record 52 points in a game, eclipsing the mark set by former Virginia star Ralph Sampson.

The creativity that makes Toliver a special point guard was apparent off the court as well. She was a trumpet player in Harrisonburg's jazz band, concert band and orchestra and was named the school's Jazz

Improvisation Player of the Year. More important to the Terps, she was the Associated Press Group AA Player of the Year as a senior.

"I encouraged Kristi that if she liked basketball, then don't just be good at it — be the best you can be," George Toliver said. "The second thing was to respect the game, to understand the game and learn the game. I used Michael Jordan as an example. At the time, there were not a lot of female role models. When she was really young, there wasn't a WNBA. I used Michael, and I said that in terms of image, of always being a quality person and great player, it was always 'Be like Mike.' The third thing to learn was to be unselfish. That means to be aware of everything that is going on in the game and to always be sharing. Selfishness will always be exposed in basketball. People will always be able to identify the selfish player, and they will always want someone who is unselfish."

Years of watching Jordan taught Toliver not to fear taking a big shot, but she wasn't naturally vocal and that had implications she was still wrestling with on and off the court as the calendar year came to a close.

Toliver began experiencing mild pain in her shins during the Paradise Jam in the Virgin Islands, and the discomfort got significantly worse in early December, eventually forcing her to miss five games during the month and limiting her to three minutes in another.

Injuries weren't the only problem. The lack of communication and organization that troubled Toliver in summer school resurfaced to the detriment of her academic performance, catching everyone by surprise.

For the first time in her life, Toliver was being pushed athletically and academically, and the adjustment wasn't easy. Outwardly, Toliver continued to exude a cool exterior, but a lack of organization was causing her to struggle with a myriad of responsibilities. She needed to reach out instead of turning inward.

The Terps returned from the Paradise Jam eager to resume practice. Instead of suffering through a post-Tennessee hangover, they were energized. The convincing win against Michigan State and the narrow loss to the Lady Vols gave Maryland a clear view of the work that needed to be done, but there were no marquee opponents in the team's immediate future. In a six-month season, December is the strangest month. The excitement accompanying a new season starts to fade, practice and game schedules are disrupted for exam week, and the holidays bring another break at month's end. From a scheduling perspective, teams are still a month away from conference play, and teams like Maryland see few games where the outcome is genuinely in doubt.

With the exception of a home game against Pac-10 opponent Arizona, the month offered the Terps a stream of competition from lower-tier conferences. The question wasn't whether Maryland would win but by how many points. While coaches are loathe to assume victory against any foe, the goal for the Terps was domination. The team couldn't be content with winning on superior skill; it had to meet Frese's exacting standards.

One of the primary objectives in December was the development of on-court continuity. After Maryland moved up to ninth in both major polls, it was easy to forget the team's inexperience. Perry, Langhorne, Newman, Toliver and Doron constituted the starting five to open the season; Coleman and Harper were the first two reserves off the bench. The freshmen, Toliver and Coleman, had much to learn despite outstanding early-season play. Harper, though a sophomore in terms of eligibility, had limited game experience because of the Achilles tendon that had cut her first season short. And after playing three games in three days in the Virgin Islands, Harper experienced soreness in her Achilles after returning to College Park. Though the soreness wasn't completely unexpected given the injury she had suffered and the intensity of the competition, Frese was taking no chances. Harper sat out Maryland's first two games in December.

Harper's absence hardly mattered in terms of the end results. On Dec. 1, the Terps welcomed Appalachian State to the Comcast Center with a blowout. Langhorne directed the opening tip to Doron and then sprinted down the middle of the court. Doron fed the ball back to Langhorne, who made a layup five seconds into the game as Maryland scored 66 first-half points. The only suspense was whether the Terps would break the school record for most points in a game. Frese made liberal use of her bench, but with Harper sitting out, she had only four players to substitute and one of them, Ross, was making a limited return from the knee injury.

The Terps shot 60 percent from the field and outrebounded the Mountaineers 54-23 to win 118-59, three points shy of the team scoring record. Six players scored at least 16 points and Perry, rebounding from a poor outing against Tennessee, contributed 16 points and 16 rebounds. Langhorne made all six of her field goal attempts for 17 points despite playing a season-low 13 minutes.

Three days later, in-state opponent Mount St. Mary's came to the Comcast Center, and the Terps were no less dominant as Langhorne made her first 10 shots en route to scoring 30 points in just 21 minutes. The best teams in the country found it hard to stop Langhorne, who was 14 of 15 from the floor against Mount St. Mary's. For the lesser teams on the schedule, it was impossible. The Terps won 102-53.

After beating Appalachian State and Mount St. Mary's, Maryland went on the road and walloped Monmouth 88-55 in a game Toliver sat out. The victory set up the one game on the December schedule that was sure to have Maryland's attention: Arizona. The year before, the Terps had gone on the road and defeated the Wildcats 84-77 in overtime. Maryland needed an eight-foot jumper at the buzzer by Perry to send the game into overtime, so there would be no looking past Arizona. The Wildcats had been struck by tragedy since the teams last met. Star center Shawntinice Polk, who made 8 of 12 shots, scored 19 points and had eight rebounds in the first game, died of a pulmonary blood clot at age 22 on Sept. 26, 2005. The passing of the team's best player was a devastating emotional blow.

Arizona was also Frese's alma mater and Wildcats coach Joan Bonvicini had led the team during Brenda's final two years. By the time Bonvicini became coach, Frese's foot problems had already taken hold and 13 years had passed since her graduation, so there wasn't a "teacher vs. student" aspect to the game. Yet relations between Frese and Bonvicini were certainly cordial.

Though Toliver, in her last game of the month, saw just three minutes, Maryland played one of its more complete games of the season. Determined to stop Langhorne, who had made 29 of 33 field goal attempts in the previous three games, Arizona sagged inside, forcing the Terps to score from the perimeter. In previous years, three-point shooting had been a problem, but even without Toliver the Terps were a much-improved shooting team. Maryland punished the Wildcats for their efforts to stop Langhorne by making 8 of 9 three-point attempts in the first half while building a 46-27 lead.

Arizona was forced to defend the perimeter with vigor in the second half, and Maryland responded by scoring 30 of its 46 points in the paint.

The Terps put on a clinic in offensive efficiency. Led by Marissa Coleman, who made 4 of 5 three-pointers and scored 20 points, Maryland shot 62.3 percent from the field for the game although Langhorne only made 5 of 12. In their most complete performance of the year to date, the Terps blasted Arizona 92-67.

    With Toliver out of the lineup, Doron moved from shooting guard to point guard, and Coleman slid into the starting lineup. Doron was the team's most experienced player and had the skill to play the point, but the transition wasn't always smooth. Maryland clobbered Coppin State 69-39 and George Mason 70-33 in the first two games of Toliver's extended absence, but the Terps were giving the ball away at an alarming rate — a problem all season. Maryland averaged 21 turnovers while Toliver was largely sidelined for four games. Doron, meanwhile, struggled against Coppin State and George Mason, shooting 7-for-26 and committing 10 turnovers. Doron's indecisiveness and tendency to overanalyze on the court was exacerbated when she was playing point full time.

    While Doron was trying to get comfortable, Toliver was still searching to find her way offcourt. She didn't reach out for help in the classroom and wasn't vigilant in rehabilitating her shin. Toliver never indicated to anyone on the coaching staff that there was a problem, and Frese was livid because Maryland has a strong academic support staff. The player counted on to lead what the Terps hoped was a Final Four team was non-communicative.

    After Toliver's struggles in summer school resurfaced, Frese called a meeting after the George Mason game. The coach maintained a good relationship with Toliver's parents and kept them apprised of what was transpiring. The Tolivers shared Frese's frustration. Toliver's problems were typical for first-semester freshmen. She could handle the academic workload but was juggling an enormous amount of responsibility for the first time in her life. Instead of letting things fester, Frese scheduled the meeting with Toliver and her parents, Laura Meckley, the team's academic advisor, and Pearson.

    Toliver was brought to task in a very intense, emotional session. That she was struggling wasn't the problem. If Toliver was going to lead a team with national championship aspirations, her teammates needed to count on her, and part of that was taking care of business in the training room and the classroom. Some of her weaknesses were being revealed, but Frese made it clear everybody cared about Toliver.

Doron embraced her leadership role, and it was never more obvious than in December. With Toliver's difficulties reaching their zenith, Doron was the person she sought out. "When I was having my stretch of going insane in December, [Doron] was the one I would talk to about it," Toliver said. "She was the one I felt most comfortable talking to about that type of stuff."

Watching Toliver negotiate her first semester was like watching the rerun of a bad television show for Doron, and she was trying to help Toliver change the channel. "I saw a lot of me in her, especially as a freshman," Doron said. "I had already made all those mistakes, so I could tell her about how I got through the trouble she was having. At some point we were calling her 'Shay 2' because she was doing everything dumb I did. I was trying to help her avoid the mistakes I made."

Doron talked with Toliver about a range of subjects, including the importance of coming to practice focused on basketball, something that was difficult if other parts of your campus life aren't in order. "When I came to practice, she knew if I had a bad day," Toliver said of Doron. "She told me, 'You can't have a bad day; you can't let social things, personal things get in the way of basketball.' Before she walks into Comcast every day, she tells herself, 'Put your game face on.' I started doing the same. If Shay is having a bad day, you will never know it."

The team scattered for Christmas following the George Mason game. Often, coaches don't allow players a break around the holidays, but Frese makes it a point to give her team a sizable rest, reasoning that her players would prefer to spend time with their families. With final exams completed and conference play on the horizon, it was a good time for a rest. The games played during the second semester often define seasons, and Frese wanted her team to approach the new year with renewed passion.

When Toliver returned from Christmas break a day earlier than most of her teammates, Frese invited her to her home to watch a Washington Wizards game. While the meeting a week earlier had been a difficult one, Frese wanted to reinforce to Toliver that she believed in her. A couple of days later, Toliver delivered a heartfelt, handwritten note telling Frese she wanted to be a player the staff and her teammates could depend on. In the last 10 days of December, Toliver, without playing a minute of basketball, turned a critical corner.

As Toliver suffered through a rocky December, one of her teammates wasn't around for part of the month. Frese allowed junior Aurelie
Noirez to return to her native Vandoeuvre, France, at the conclusion of
exams. The move was a little unconventional — players typically miss
games only in emergencies — but such empathy summed up what
Maryland's players like about Frese.

Noirez arrived in College Park as part of Frese's first recruiting
class, but outwardly she had little in common with highly touted classmates Doron and France. Noirez was signed without Frese seeing her
play. Walz saw her at the European Championships in 2001 and the
Terps, in need of post players, offered her a scholarship. Noirez, who
wanted to come to the United States to play and gain an education, glad-
ly accepted. She arrived in America with a limited grasp of the English
language, particularly its nuances. In Noirez's first team meeting,
Fingers told players to arrive in shape because she was going to run
them hard.

"Aurelie came up to us after the meeting and said, 'I don't understand meeting, but I know I'm going to die on Monday,' " Frese recalled
with a laugh.

Confusion over what the strength and conditioning coach was going
to do aside, Noirez made a smooth transition. She excelled in the classroom and made friends easily, but after remaining in the United States
for Christmas her freshman season, Noirez battled homesickness in
January. Unlike teammates whose parents attend games or are a long-
distance phone call away, Noirez's communication with her family is
limited primarily to e-mail and text messaging. Making a decision based
on common sense instead of basketball sense, Frese allowed Noirez to
return home for eight days.

The entire team reconvened for practice on Dec. 27 to begin preparation for the Terrapin Classic, an annual four-team tournament held at
Maryland. With a tournament field of Central Connecticut State,
Maryland-Eastern Shore and Furman, two victories were automatic for
the Terps. With Toliver nursing shin problems, Maryland coaches
increasingly gave Coleman a chance to run the point. The 6-foot-1
Coleman, with broad shoulders and a powerful body, doesn't look like a
classic point guard. Instead, she's part of a new breed of women's bas-

ketball players.

A decade ago, 7-foot male players were expected to play with their back to the basket. Big guys who wanted to shoot from the perimeter were derided as soft. Along came the Kevin Garnetts and Dirk Nowitzkis and the expectations of what big players should and shouldn't do started to change. Coleman is that type of player in the women's game. Physically, she is big enough to play in the paint, and the 8.1 rebounds Coleman grabbed per game provided ample evidence of her work. But she is also capable of playing point guard and was a stellar 47 percent shooter from three-point range for the season. Coleman has the size to overpower smaller guards, plus the shot and agility to take bigger players away from the basket. And the gregarious Coleman relished the opportunity to run the team.

The break and Coleman's presence to alleviate some of the ball-handling responsibility seemed to spark Doron. In the opening game of the Terrapin Classic, Maryland clubbed Central Connecticut State 94-57 as both Doron and Coleman enjoyed strong games. Doron made 4 of 6 three-pointers and equaled her season high with 26 points. Coleman scored a then-career-high 22 points on 7 of 9 shooting and had 6 rebounds and 6 assists. Langhorne, continuing her torrid shooting run, made all nine of her shots, scored 22 points and grabbed 10 rebounds in 22 minutes.

The championship game against Furman was almost a carbon copy of the Central Connecticut State contest. Maryland limited the Paladins to 28.6 percent shooting in the first half and raced to a 44-20 lead at the break. Doron scored 26 points for the second game in a row, gaining tournament MVP honors, and Coleman stuffed the box score with 16 points, 10 rebounds and 5 assists. Harper's sore Achilles tendon was long forgotten as she finished with 13 points and 10 boards in the 92-58 win.

Frese challenged her team to dominate December at the beginning of the month, and it won eight games by an average of 37.6 points. The closest game was the 25-point win over Arizona.

As 2005 gave way to 2006, Maryland was 12-1 and ranked sixth in the nation. Toliver was feeling better every day and eager to return to the court. Six weeks into the season, ACC play beckoned. A team's character is revealed in conference play when the talent level is similar and the opponents are familiar ones. There aren't any secrets — in most any league in the country — and the ACC was stronger than it had ever been.

The Terps would begin learning a lot more about themselves in a matter of days.

Chapter 6

"I'm Going to Die for a Recruit"

Winters in Minnesota can be as foreboding as any in the nation. With an average January temperature of 8 degrees and snowfall totals up to 70 inches a year, it's not a place for someone unprepared. A trip to upstate Minnesota in the middle of winter, when temperatures are routinely sub-zero and the snowfall soars above state averages, normally would be dependent on the weather forecast. But normal isn't a word used to describe Frese's meteoric rise through the coaching ranks.

Still just 36 entering the 2006-07 season, Frese has seven years of head coaching experience, four NCAA Tournament appearances and a national title to her credit. The root of that success can be traced to her ability to identify and recruit high school girls who are going to be successful at the college level, an aspect of the game in which she has had few peers. Frese is charismatic, confident, young and attractive, all factors that work in her favor as she builds relationships with prospective recruits and their families.

For all of her personality, what makes Frese a great recruiter is her enjoyment of the process and work ethic. If a person Frese trusts gives her a tip, she explores it with an open mind. Frese works as hard at recruiting as she does preparing for a game, and the recruiting wins and losses can be just as exhilarating and deflating. In her first four years at Maryland, Frese routinely landed recruiting classes ranked among the nation's best.

Nothing bespeaks Frese's tenacity on the recruiting trail better than an episode in the winter of 1996. Just 25, an age many coaches are wrapping up a master's degree and hoping to land a full-time position, Frese was the first-year recruiting coordinator at Iowa State. It was a position of great importance — the Cyclones are a member of the Big 12

Conference — particularly for someone with just two years of Division I coaching experience. The pressure to recruit players and win in a league like the Big 12 is enormous, and Iowa State coach Bill Fennelly entrusted one of the most important aspects of his program to a young woman barely old enough to rent a car.

Fennelly and Frese caught word of a junior in Minnesota who was on pace to shatter the state's all-time scoring record, for both girls and boys, the only complicating factor being that she lived in Roseau, Minn., about 10 miles from the Canadian border. The travel wasn't easy and the competition far from great, but Frese wasn't going to wait until the summer AAU circuit to discover whether Megan Taylor could play. She flew from Ames, Iowa, home of the Cyclones, to Grand Forks, N.D., rented a car and drove nearly two hours to the gym. Frese wanted to make the best of the opportunity Fennelly had given her, and the weather wasn't going to be a deterrent.

She arrived in the tiny gym and her Iowa State gear attracted attention from the fans. After the initial curiosity about the Cyclones recruiting one of their own subsided, people told Frese they couldn't believe she came to the game and she certainly couldn't leave afterward. The forecast called for a nasty snowstorm, even by Minnesota standards, to pass through the area. Frese didn't pay much attention. She had a job to do and a flight to catch back in Grand Forks the next morning. Either way, there wasn't a hotel in Roseau to stay in.

She was there to see Taylor, and from the minute the 5-11 forward walked onto the court, Frese knew she was a player. She made three-pointers, ran the point and posted people up. Frese got goosebumps watching her play and imagining the possibilities. She couldn't wait to get somewhere with cell phone service, which was much spottier in 1996, to call Fennelly. Unable to talk to Taylor, she told her coach to relay word that Iowa State wanted her to be a Cyclone. Without ever consulting Fennelly, she assured Taylor's coach that Iowa State's head man soon would be on hand to see the young star play.

For two hours during the game, Frese bordered on being giddy, knowing she was watching a future star and she was the first big-time college coach on Taylor's trail. This situation was everything Frese could have hoped for. Then she walked outside. The locals and the weathermen were right about the predicted snow. Frese started heading back to Grand Forks in near white-out conditions. If Taylor's performance made her a dream recruit, driving in the snow was a nightmare.

Though visibility was beyond poor, she was able to follow a tractor trailer, but the excitement of watching Taylor play gave way to a more primal emotion. "I've never been so scared in my life," Frese said. "I kept saying to myself, 'I'm going to die for a recruit.' I didn't know where the road was, and I knew if I pulled over I was stuck. I was going on blind faith [behind the truck]. If he had gone into a ditch, I would have gone right in with him."

After more than four hours of white-knuckle driving, Frese arrived at her hotel and pried her hands off the steering wheel. Despite getting back, she didn't catch her flight because it was canceled. An area accustomed to working through snowstorms the way folks in Maryland push through a severe thunderstorm closed schools the following day.

When Frese called Fennelly the next morning, she relayed one important message: You need to get Megan Taylor on the phone and offer her a scholarship and, by the way, I survived a horrific snowstorm.

In the summer between her junior and senior seasons, Taylor erupted. A girl from a town with a population of less than 3,000 emerged as a highly coveted recruit, and Iowa State had a six-month head start in her recruitment. Taylor committed to the Cyclones and went on to become the school's all-time leading scorer. As her star rose, so too did that of the young assistant who recruited her.

Big-time college basketball is the most public of games. From Midnight Madness to the NCAA Tournament, television coverage is heavy. With its fast pace and small court, basketball makes for compelling viewing. There are no helmets or hats to cover faces and mask emotions. From fury to unbridled joy, the emotions, gyrations and gesticulations of players and coaches often are the focal point of roving TV cameras. More so than any other sport, basketball is an intimate game, and that is one of its primary attractions. It's easy for fans to feel as if they know the personalities of the players and coaches involved.

While every inch of the court is within the scope of the camera, the most important component of building a successful program — recruiting — isn't seen by anybody. From John Wooden and Dean Smith to Pat Summitt and Geno Auriemma, coaches who win are lauded for their sideline wizardry, and much of it is deserved. But for all the work a coach dedicates to game-planning, scouting and refining a style of play, greatness starts with the ability to recruit. Wooden won for a lot of reasons, not the least of which was the presence of Lew Alcindor, Bill

Walton and friends. UConn and Tennessee won on the women's side because they had the likes of Diana Taurasi and Tamika Catchings.

Players win games, and Frese has proven she is as good as anyone in the country at attracting talent. Her success on the recruiting trail has gained attention. The obvious question everybody asks is, how does she do it? The answer is twofold.

First, Frese works at a university that is easy to sell to recruits and for an athletic director committed to excellence. With its urban setting, state-of-the-art arena and excellent academics, Maryland offers everything a basketball coach could ask for. It's ironic that since Frese has taken over in College Park, Maryland is often referred to as a "top-five" job for the aforementioned reasons. If it's really a top-five job, then no one should be surprised when Maryland recruits at a top-five level.

Second and most important, Frese is able to connect with the kids she is recruiting. She does so in large part by learning as much as she can about a prospective recruit, talking to high school and AAU coaches, parents, and anybody else who can provide useful insight. Learning about a prospect's likes and dislikes makes it easier for Frese to engage in meaningful conversation and allows her to get a better feel for the prospect's character. For all the skill on the Maryland roster, Frese doesn't recruit strictly on talent. She wants players who will fit in with her program, which helps explain the incredible chemistry of the 2006 team.

The recruits Maryland pursues with the most fervor are the ones the staff feels will be an asset on the court and in the locker room. On hot July days when Frese is traveling across the country during the NCAA observation period, watching countless AAU games, she looks beyond points and rebounds. How does a player interact with her teammates? Does she look at her coach in the huddle during timeouts? Those are the moments that reveal a player's character, and Frese doesn't want to miss those clues.

"Work ethic will take you a long way, even if you have lesser ability," she said. "You can see it on the floor. Is she diving for loose balls or competing for rebounds? [Recruiting is about] weeding through [to find] kids that are committed."

Once Frese identifies a player she wants, the Terps are relentless in their pursuit. Unlike a lot of programs that assign assistants to geographic areas or groups of players, Maryland uses its entire staff to recruit a prospect. All the members of the Terps' recruiting team have contact in one form or another to increase the player's comfort level. Frese feels it's important — and beneficial for both parties — for players to know the entire staff.

Maryland's recruiting team shares information to make sure correspondence isn't repetitive, and if something important happens, they can all acknowledge it. The Terps don't overwhelm recruits with mail, e-mail or text messages, but prospective recruits receive approximately three types of correspondence per week. Sometimes the letter or e-mail may contain a quote of the day, other times a joke referencing previous communication. The Maryland staff lets players know they are interested and following their progress, but don't bombard them with information to the point where the prospects stop reading what's sent.

Another important component of the Terps' success on the court and the recruiting trail is the staff's willingness to listen. The players on the team and recruits provide coaches with a lot of information, if they are listening to what is being said. Engaging in one-sided conversation or correspondence with a recruit is counterproductive. Bernabei was recruiting a girl who eliminated a team from her list of possible schools because it sent her reams of faxes at school although she hated receiving them. It sounds like a minor inconvenience, but somebody wasn't listening.

Floyd, Walz and Bernabei can't be underestimated in the recruiting process because Frese can't be everywhere all the time. But Frese is the face of the Maryland program, and her willingness to work on the recruiting trail is what helps set her apart. Recruiting isn't glamorous and television commentators don't shower coaches with praise for being in muggy high school gymnasiums, but she works as hard at it as she does under the bright lights of the arena.

Once a program reaches a certain status, it often recruits itself, allowing head coaches to step back, at least slightly, from the recruiting process. The head coach becomes, in sales terms, the closer. That hasn't and likely won't happen at Maryland. Frese is as involved in recruiting as any head coach in the nation. The morning after the Terps upset No. 1 North Carolina during the regular season, she hopped on a plane and flew to Indiana to scout a player. College coaching staffs can make a limited number of phone calls, per NCAA rules, to prospective recruits, but high school players can call coaches anytime. It's not unusual for Maryland recruiting targets to have Frese's cell phone number, and they can expect her to answer the phone. She doesn't pawn recruiting work off on her assistants and then swoop in for a cameo like a star actor making a guest appearance.

"As far as the personality and steam behind [our recruiting], she definitely generates it," Bernabei said. "In the gym watching, on the phone, e-mailing, texting, the bottom line is I tell kids, and I believe it — you are going to love Brenda Frese, that is who you are going to play for and she is going to be here. . . . I'm selling the program, but I'm definitely selling her, and I know she is going to follow through. One of our primary things in the process is recruiting kids with good character, and I know she is going to be able to relate to them."

Frese has a natural charisma that allows her to relate to people, and her age and experiences as a player provide a unique perspective that benefits her immensely. She was 31 when accepting the Maryland job and out of college herself for less than 10 years. When you are 17, the age of 31 can seem like 71, but Frese's experiences remain fresh in her mind. She wasn't a McDonald's All-American coming out of Washington High School in Cedar Rapids, Iowa, but she was an all-state performer who attracted considerable attention. Frese pared her list of potential colleges to Arizona, Indiana and Alabama-Birmingham so she knows how difficult it is to tell coaches you won't be attending their schools. Frese also remembered what it was like to be recruited, what stood out to her, what she disliked and which factors that helped her make a decision.

Frese flew from Cedar Rapids, Iowa to her college of choice, the University of Arizona, leaving home for the first time. She suffered career-ending foot injuries that resulted in throbbing pain for more than a year so she knows what it's like to be homesick and how difficult major injuries are to overcome. Frese doesn't talk about her personal experiences with recruits, figuring they could care less about her adventures as a high school and college athlete, but those memories remain fresh enough that she doesn't forget the lessons.

The higher coaches ascend on the coaching ladder, naturally the more important they become. Media demands grow and strangers emerge to offer their congratulations. Frese fulfills nearly every media request possible and is always polite to fans, but she is devoid of the baggage that typically accompanies rising fame. She doesn't take herself too seriously and isn't afraid to have fun at her own expense.

When Bernabei was interviewing for a vacant assistant coaching position at Maryland, Frese took her to Baltimore's Inner Harbor for dinner. By the time dinner ended, it was raining and there wasn't an umbrella in sight. Determined to stay as dry as possible, Frese told Bernabei they should make a run for it, the only problem being the run didn't last long. Frese took a few steps and tumbled down a set of stairs. Bernabei's first thought was one of concern, what if Frese was hurt? She didn't have a cell phone and certainly didn't know her way around Baltimore. Fortunately, the only thing wounded may have been Frese's pride, but it was tough to tell as she sat on the ground covered in water laughing all the while.

After she accepted the job, Bernabei told the story to a prospective recruit, who thought it was hilarious. Everybody falls and people laugh, assuming an injury isn't suffered, but Frese possesses perhaps the most important trait — the ability to laugh at herself.

Though Frese doesn't act as if the world owes her something, she won't be mistaken for passive. Frese is respectful of what others have accomplished, but doesn't defer to anybody. With the support of an athletic director committed to providing her with the resources to win, Frese expected to sign the best players in the nation and eventually win the game's biggest prize when coming to Maryland.

"When [Frese] was recruiting me, she knew she was going to win a national championship," Coleman said. "She was confident in that and as a recruit, you feed off her confidence and ultimately want to be a part of that.

"She's not like other coaches telling you what you want to hear. She's honest with you, and you can tell she sincerely cares about you as more than just a player. She has a great personality for it. She's not stiff, she likes to have fun and joke and that helps. . . . A lot of places would tell you this is the place for you. Coach B wouldn't do that. She wouldn't tell you where you should go. She would tell you, 'I want you to come here, but I want you to go where you think you will fit in best.' "

With a roster that could serve as a McDonald's All-American alumni team, Frese's recruiting successes outweigh the failures, but it's an unpredictable part of the business. Like any coach, she has had her share of forgettable moments, some pass harmlessly while others reverberate.

Depending on how many scholarships they have to offer in a given year, the Terps tend to focus on a group of 20 to 30 players and winnow the list as time and circumstances dictate. Frese and her staff try to know what type of prospect they are recruiting and whether the interest they are expressing is mutual, which makes the story of what happened with one target with a connection to the university, all the more bizarre.

Floyd and Frese were preparing to fly to Southern California for a home visit with a prospect in the class of 2005. The recruit, who had ties to the university, left a message the day before the visit saying she needed to reschedule. With the plane tickets booked and a full schedule over the coming weeks, that was nearly impossible. Floyd called the girl's house and spoke to her father, telling him they couldn't reschedule on less than 24 hours notice. Neither the father nor the recruit called back, and Frese and Floyd boarded the flight and headed to California, assuming their target would make the meeting she helped arrange.

When they arrived at the recruit's house, she was nowhere to be found. Frese and Floyd went through with the home visit, figuring if they went all the way out there they might as well make the presentation, though their enthusiasm was on the wane. The recruit's father was eventually able to get in touch with her via cell phone — she was getting her hair done. The trip cost Maryland a couple thousand dollars, invaluable time and extreme aggravation, but at the very least, they knew who they didn't want.

Generally, recruiting is an amicable process, with coaches developing closer relationships with certain players while others remain distant, but either way, both sides are cordial. Even if a player's interest in a school isn't strong, the coach and likely an assistant will make their presentation, showering the player with attention and with the offer of a full scholarship on the table, something most players and parents appreciate. But that's not always the case.

Maryland's 2004 recruiting class, buoyed by Langhorne and Harper, was rated second in the nation, but it could've been stronger. The Terps were in pursuit of other top players in the class, including one they initially thought might come to College Park.

Frese, accompanied by Bernabei, thought the first home visit with the highly regarded player went well. She left believing there was a real chance the recruit would help her build a champion at Maryland. In the ensuing months, the relationship between Frese and the player remained strong, but the Terps coach felt a strain growing between her and the recruit's mother. Some coaches recruit the player, some recruit parents or other influential people in the recruiting process — it's part of the business. After the player pariticpated in an individual camp at another school competing for her services, a chill began to descend on the relationship between Frese and the player's mother, and that was the backdrop for the second home visit with the highly regarded prospect on the final day of the recruiting period.

The mother had made dinner for every coach that had come by for a home visit, but when Frese arrived, only the recruit and her father were downstairs for the first 30 minutes. When the mother came strolling down the stairs, she was clad in the colors of an opposing school and barely acknowledged the presence of Frese and Walz, who accompanied her on the visit. Food was eventually put on the table, but she treated her guests from Maryland with an emotion bordering on contempt. After finishing an uneasy meal, Frese walked through her presentation outlining why Maryland would be the right fit for the recruit, and when she finished, there were no questions.

The mother got out of her seat, walked around the table, picked up a black bag and said, "Now I'm going to tell you why my daughter isn't going to Maryland." She proceeded to show Frese a telephone bill with calls to College Park marked and accused Maryland of making calls to her daughter in violation of NCAA rules.

Frese's blood reached an immediate boil. She quickly pointed out that the piece of paper she was holding detailed outgoing calls, and it was perfectly legal for her or anybody on her staff to accept calls from prospective recruits. Frese was stunned. She would not have been doing her job if she hadn't answered the player's calls, but on a much more personal level, the allegations were an attack on her character and one she wasn't going to let pass. In hindsight, if Frese had it to do all over again, she would have thanked them for their time and left, but that's not her nature. The conversation became heated, so much so that the créme-colored pants Frese wore to the visit had a black spot on the shin from where Walz had been kicking her under the table. The player, a kid Frese had grown fond of, wasn't going to wear a Maryland uniform, but her mother wasn't going to attack Frese and her program without a response.

After the most contentious home visit of their careers, Frese and Walz got in their car still shocked over what had transpired. Moments after the Maryland coaches pulled away from her house, Frese's cell phone rang — it was a prospective recruit calling to talk. She howled in laughter before picking up the phone.

––––––––––––

The recruiting success Maryland has enjoyed since Frese's arrival has rankled some in the game. After consecutive top five classes and the addition of Tennessee transfer Sa'de Wiley-Gatewood, never mind the fact she contacted Maryland, the attention about how the Terps attracted the nation's top players began to grow. There were newspaper accounts involving the Terps' recruiting practices.

For their part, Maryland was told by the NCAA that a couple of high profile women's basketball coaches called to lodge complaints about its recruiting. The legislative body came to the university in what Maryland officials described as routine discussion and follow up in the recruitment of high profile athletes. The NCAA apparently uncovered nothing of substance because it never sent the Terps a letter of inquiry or alleged any misconduct.

From the Terrapins' perspective, any innuendo was simply sour grapes.

"You are naïve when you grow up and think things are a certain way," Frese said. "Then you get into the mix and you are recruiting the same players as the heavy hitters [and things change]. I feel like we've done things the right way and then they attack your character. I've been accused of anything and everything over the last four years, more than I ever imagined. But when you've done things the right way and had those values instilled in you, and your character is attacked behind the scenes, that is amazing. When I stuck my nose in there, it was like she must be doing something wrong. Plain and simple, we just outworked them and showed the kids we cared about them."

The rise of 24-hour news networks and the Internet have changed the media. There was a time when rumor wasn't typically reported, particularly when there was no supporting evidence beyond anonymous accusations. For better or worse, that age has long since passed. As the Terps were making their way up the polls, articles referencing alleged recruiting missteps began to appear more frequently, though the closest thing anybody had to evidence was the word of disgruntled coaches who refused to be named. There was little Maryland could do to combat the rumors other than profess their innocence, something that doesn't attract nearly as much attention as a coach benefiting from the Terps taking a public relations hit while hiding behind the veil of anonymity.

Publicly, the Terps took the high road, saying jealousy is a byproduct of success, but privately the public relations beating they were taking stung.

"I think she outworks people and that makes a lot of people mad," Bernabei said of Frese's critics. "She makes it hard on everybody else in this profession that is at her level. A lot of people making her money don't want to do the grind anymore because they've just spent 30 years doing it and they have their assistants do it. She's not about that. That's why she is going to be successful.

"It's frustrating. You tell yourself if we weren't doing things right, people wouldn't be talking about us. You can always say those positive things, but yeah, it's hurtful. It does frustrate you because we work really hard. We put in the hours. Instead of having people say look at how Maryland does it, they say they must be doing something wrong and that gets old."

The Maryland players found the idea of Frese doing anything different than other schools misguided.

"It really does bother me," Langhorne said. "It's just a shame because Coach B put in so much work to get these recruits here and people are just jealous. That's how we see it. Why did we come to Maryland? Because we didn't want to go to a traditional program that has won a lot of championships. We wanted to do something new."

Chapter 7

"We Should Thank Duke"

After Maryland wrapped up its late-morning shoot-around at Boston College's Conte Forum in January, Frese called the players into the center circle. Three days earlier, the Terps had routed Manhattan 82-49 to conclude a stretch of soft non-conference games.

With the start of ACC play just hours away, Frese told the players they had reason to feel good. Maryland's practices had been crisp and its play sharp, but the level of competition was going to rise considerably now, a challenge everyone was ready to face.

The Terps boarded their charter bus back to the hotel knowing the pregame meal was scheduled for 2:30 p.m. The tight schedule made the long ride all the stranger. The bus driver was giving the Terps a tour of the city, pointing out where the Boston Massacre occurred and the location of the bar that inspired the long running TV series "Cheers." Maryland's players were sitting on the bus wondering why it was taking so long to get to the hotel. Only one player, Coleman, had any inkling as to what was going on.

In 2006, Boston was much more than merely the home of the newest member of the ACC, Boston College. The city represented something much bigger, and Frese wanted her team to be aware of the significance. Boston was the home of the Final Four, the biggest event in women's basketball, and the place where the Terps dreamed of playing in four months.

Coaches stress to not look ahead ad nauseum, and Frese isn't any different, making the trip to the TD Banknorth Garden, a facility opened in 1995 to replace the famed Boston Garden, a risky gambit. Hours before playing 19th-ranked Boston College in the conference opener for both teams, Frese wanted to show her team what it was working toward. The building's awkward name — courtesy of the arena's corporate partner, a charmless necessity needed to offset rising costs in the world of sports — didn't diminish the building's grandeur. TD Banknorth Garden, home of the NBA's Boston Celtics and the National Hockey League's Boston Bruins, held 18,854 for basketball games.

As the Terps went up a flight of steps entering the building, the players who figured out what was going on with Coleman's help joked about meeting the Celtics, but Frese didn't have the NBA on her mind.

"I don't think we had really put Boston in perspective. This is where the Final Four is played — the championship," Harper said. "Her taking us there was like, 'We can do this, guys.' Coach B believes in us way more than we believe in ourselves. She was like, 'Do you guys realize this is where we can be in a couple of months if we handle our business?' "

The Bruins were playing that night, so ice covered the arena floor, but the Terps got the message. They sat in the stands, admiring the 16 championship banners the Celtics had earned while envisioning the opportunity to win a title of their own.

"I know Coach B and she loves motivational tactics, and it took an extra 30 minutes to get back to the hotel, so I just figured [we were going to the Garden]," Coleman said. "Sitting in the arena hearing Coach B talk, and the confidence she had in this team, she knew we could be in the Final Four. Just looking at my teammates, we all looked at each other, and I think everybody got goose bumps at that point, because we knew we wanted to play in that arena and we were capable of getting there."

Before Maryland could think about returning to Boston, the Terps needed to prove they could win on the road against upper-tier competition. The Eagles, invited to join the ACC as part of the league's football-induced expansion, presented Maryland with its first real challenge since the Tennessee game in November. Boston College was 12-2 and had a starting lineup of three seniors and two juniors. Maryland and Boston College couldn't have been more different. The Terps were young and athletic and wanted to push the ball at every opportunity. The Eagles relied on experience and defense to grind out low-scoring victories. Maryland was second in the ACC and the nation in scoring, while Boston College was second in the league in scoring defense (58.7

points).

The Eagles and Terps engaged in a slugfest from the start, with both teams struggling to score. The Terps trailed by six points early in the game but, led by Langhorne and Harper, controlled the paint for a 29-23 halftime lead. The second half was more of the same. Maryland scored just two points in the first four minutes and Boston College drained consecutive three-pointers to tie the game, and neither team was able to build a working margin. After Newman hit a three-pointer to cut Maryland's deficit to 42-40, nobody led by more than three points in the final 12:22 of regulation.

After clobbering nine consecutive opponents, the Terps were involved in a test of nerves on the road against a legitimate top 20 team (Boston College later advanced to the Sweet 16 before falling to Utah in the NCAA Tournament). Trailing 56-55, Harper made a short jumper to give Maryland a 57-56 lead with 2:00 to go. Boston College's Brooke Queenan, a second-team all-ACC performer who shot 80 percent from the line, made the second of two free throws 53 seconds later to tie the game 57-57, but neither team scored again in regulation. The Terps, who outrebounded Boston College 51-38, took three shots on their next possession but were unable to convert any including a layup by Coleman with four seconds left. Despite Coleman's miss, Frese was pleased to see her cutting to the basket, wanting the ball with the game on the line. After Boston College's desperation three-point attempt failed to find the basket, Maryland was heading into its first overtime game of the season and the fifth of the Frese era.

The Terps revived their offense — 57 points was their lowest 40-minute output of the season. Harper knocked the tip to Coleman who immediately fired the ball to the sprinting Langhorne for a layup two seconds into overtime. Kindyll Dorsey answered with a three-pointer 22 seconds later, giving the Eagles a one-point lead, but Langhorne, who finished with 24 points and 13 rebounds, both game highs, made a layup and converted a free throw to give Maryland the lead for good at 62-60.

The Terps had trouble distancing themselves from Boston College until Doron, who had made just one of her last seven shots, sank a three-pointer with the shot clock winding down to give Maryland a 65-61 lead with 57 seconds remaining. Dorsey's sixth three-pointer again cut the Terps lead to one, but Doron made two free throws to push the margin back to three, and the Eagles were unable to convert a last-second three-pointer.

Despite not playing its best game, Maryland defeated a quality team on the road. The Terps were 1-0 in ACC play, and the game every player, coach and fan had circled on the schedule was next.

    The Maryland-Duke rivalry has its roots in the men's game and stretches back decades. The 1980 men's ACC Tournament championship, a 73-72 Maryland loss, still burns long-time Terps fans. In Greensboro, N.C., the heart of Tobacco Road, Maryland's Buck Williams soared to the basket on his way to an apparent game-winning tip-in when he was undercut by Kenny Dennard. But the officials called no foul, and Maryland coach Lefty Driesell was again denied an ACC title.

    The rivalry reached its zenith early in the 21st century. The Maryland and Duke men were battling for ACC and national supremacy, locking up in classic duels. Fans of both schools won't quickly forget the 10-point lead Maryland blew in the final 54 seconds against Duke in 2002 or the 22-point lead the Terps squandered in the Final Four the same year. One year later, Steve Blake famously stole the ball from an inattentive Jason Williams and went in for a layup just before the half, sending Maryland fans into a frenzy and the Terps to an upset of the top-ranked Blue Devils.

    With its pristine image and some would say holier-than-thou attitude, Duke became public enemy No. 1 for Maryland fans, who didn't have to look hard to find conspiracy or deceit lurking around every corner when the Blue Devils were involved. The level of vitriol that permeated the men's basketball rivalry was mostly missing on the women's side. A true rivalry typically needs something resembling equality on the court, and that element was lacking when it came to the women's teams. While the Terps women were dominating the ACC throughout the 1980s and into the early 1990s, the Blue Devils offered little resistance. Maryland won the first 11 games between the two schools and 26 of the first 31.

    In 1992, the balance of power between the two schools began to change. Coming off two national titles by the men's program, Duke hired a young coach named Gail Goestenkors to breathe life into its women's program. The hire turned out to be a good one. After going 12-15 and 16-11 her first two seasons, Goestenkors and the Blue Devils turned the corner during the 1993-1994 season, going 22-9 and reaching the second round of the NCAA Tournament. It started a streak of 12 consecutive tournament appearances and was Duke's first step in becoming a marquee program. The Blue Devils continued to ascend, reaching the national championship game in 1999 and returning to the Final Four in 2002 and 2003. Duke entered the 2005-06 season having won at least 30 games five straight years and hadn't won fewer than 28 since the 1997-98 campaign. On any list of the premier programs in the women's game, Duke didn't rank far behind anyone but Tennessee and UConn.

As the Blue Devils continued to improve, the Terps slipped into a malaise until Frese's arrival. The team wasn't a bottom feeder, but struggled to achieve anything greater than mediocrity. Making Duke's ascent all the more painful for close followers of the Maryland program was the Blue Devils' ability to recruit the talent-laden areas surrounding College Park. The 2005-06 Duke team had three local players, including Monique Currie, the reigning ACC Player of the Year and a consensus all-American, and Wanisha Smith, the starting shooting guard.

When Frese accepted the Maryland job, there was no women's rivalry to speak of, no matter how many taut, emotion-filled games the men's teams played. Frese's goal was to turn the Terps into a national power, and that meant knocking the Blue Devils off their perch. In her first year, Maryland played Duke twice and lost by a combined 91 points.

The Terps used Duke as a measuring stick and they had a lot of growing to do just to reach the point of being competitive, but Frese wasn't daunted by the challenge. In her second year, the Terps lost the first game at Duke by 30 points, but they showed progress in the second meeting, cutting their margin of defeat to 13 points. The following season, with Frese's first two recruiting classes on board, the two teams met three times, Maryland losing by three and 11 in the regular season before getting crushed by 30 in the ACC Tournament.

Duke had beaten Maryland 12 consecutive times as their Jan. 8, 2006, confrontation loomed. As the talent level on the Maryland team increased, Frese wanted its fans to embrace Duke as a rival, and she was successful. Though attendance numbers for the Maryland women weren't great, people were aware of the team's improvement, and Frese and her players labored relentlessly to attract fans. Their efforts were working, at least when Duke came to town. Nearly a year earlier on Feb. 13, 2005, an ACC women's record crowd of 17,243 showed up at the Comcast Center for a 60-49 Duke victory.

Now, for the first time in years, there was legitimate reason to believe the Terps had the talent to beat the Blue Devils, who were ranked second in the nation. In years past, Frese didn't feel as if everybody on her team genuinely believed they could beat the Blue Devils, but that wasn't the case now. With a television audience watching, No. 6 Maryland would have the opportunity to consolidate a road win against Boston College with the program's biggest win in years.

There were just three days between the Boston College and Duke games, which was a blessing and a curse. The Terps were again expecting a huge crowd although students were still on break, and preparations for playing Duke are different. Media interest increases exponentially, additional ticket requests spike and time demands, particularly on Frese, soar. But nobody surrounding the program was complaining. Maryland was working to create an atmosphere like the one surrounding the Duke men's game.

On the court, Frese returned to defense, telling her team in an upbeat practice the day before the game the outcome hinged on making it difficult for the Blue Devils to score. Both teams would have enough offense to win; the deciding factor would be who had enough defense. Instead of having her team spend the night before thinking about Duke, Frese invited the team to her house for its annual Christmas party. It wasn't practical to hold the party before Christmas because of Noirez's absence at the end of exam week, and newlyweds Frese and Thomas — they married on Aug. 20, 2005 — were still settling into a new home. Immediately after returning from Christmas break, Maryland played four games in seven days, so a late Christmas party made sense. If the party temporarily alleviated any pre-Duke pressure, so much the better.

The Christmas gathering had become an annual tradition for the Terps since Frese's arrival. Each class was responsible for a portion of the meal: the freshmen made dessert, the sophomores prepared fajitas, the juniors concocted the appetizers — though Doron wasn't pleased with the less-than-ripe avocados — and the seniors made salads. With the exception of Coleman and Toliver splattering cake batter on the floor in a mishap involving a mixer and a good-natured argument over who was at fault, the evening contained little unexpected excitement. On the night before the biggest game of the season, the Terps made one another dinner, dropped food on their coach's new hardwood floor, and laughed the evening away, just like any other group of college friends.

What made the players different than their schoolmates was their ability to perform on the court and attract 16,097 people to the Comcast Center the following day.

As Maryland's sophomore class worked diligently to make their fajitas the best course of the meal, they were joined by an unexpected guest. Sa'de Wiley-Gatewood, who hit the shot that gave Tennessee the lead for good in its Paradise Jam showdown with the Terps, decided to transfer at the conclusion of the first semester. The 2004 Parade National Girls High School Player of the Year, Wiley-Gatewood had been one of the nation's most talented recruits, but there was never any doubt about where she was going to attend college. The Pomona, Calif., native committed to Tennessee as a freshman in high school and remained firm in her pledge. Between the time she committed and the time she arrived in Knoxville, Wiley-Gatewood collected just about every honor that could be bestowed on a girls' high school basketball player. She was on every significant all-American team and collected MVP honors at AAU camps across the nation. She was the first freshman, boy or girl, ever invited to the Nike All-American camp.

Attending Tennessee was Wiley-Gatewood's dream, and she was part of the team's ballyhooed 2004 recruiting class. But the reality at Tennessee didn't measure up to the dream. The transition from Pomona, a suburb of Los Angeles, to Knoxville provided a significant dose of culture shock, and her freshman year was derailed by a bout of patellar tendinitis that limited her to 13 games. Her second season seemed to be going much smoother — she was No. 1 ranked Tennessee's starting point guard and averaging 8.0 points and 1.3 assists. On the surface, things appeared to be good for Wiley-Gatewood, but she was a player that thrived in the open court. Her forte was penetrating to the basket; she was an improvisational wizard with the ball, capable of dishing behind the back passes and finding seams in the defense that could bring the crowd to its feet.

But Lady Vols coach Pat Summitt, who has won more than 900 games, prefers a more structured brand of basketball. Summitt controls the game from the bench while her talented point guard favored a more free-flowing game. The resulting clashes left Wiley-Gatewood, who never visited a campus other than Tennessee on a recruiting trip, more than a little unhappy. The decision to transfer was a difficult one for

Wiley-Gatewood, who didn't sleep the night before telling Summitt, but she was resolute.

What Wiley-Gatewood didn't anticipate was the public reaction to her decision, which was immediate and harsh. Wiley-Gatewood was branded as selfish in media accounts and on harsh fan message boards. The notion that the starting point guard for the No. 1 team in America would transfer was mind-boggling for most. For the person making the decision, it was about more than the team's ranking.

"I was just unhappy there," Wiley-Gatewood said. "The way I played wasn't the style of play Pat wanted. She wouldn't allow me to play the way she recruited me. I'm a penetrator; I like to push the ball and have fun. . . . It hurt me. It hurt Pat because she committed herself to me. I waited so long to get there; it was my dream school. It was hard leaving my teammates."

No matter the difficulty of the decision, Wiley-Gatewood felt it was one that needed to be made. Initially, she was expected to transfer to North Carolina or Oklahoma. Busy with her own team, Frese paid little attention to Wiley-Gatewood at the outset. As she began to consider a new college destination, Wiley-Gatewood kept returning to the game in the Virgin Islands and the fun Maryland seemed to be having. After an official visit to Oklahoma, the Sooners seemed destined to be her next team, but her father contacted the Maryland basketball staff.

Given Wiley-Gatewood's credentials coming out of high school, and the type of game she played against the Terps in the Virgin Islands, Frese felt she owed it to the program to do her due diligence on Wiley-Gatewood. Like everyone else, Frese read the reports of a selfish player leaving the Tennessee program, but Frese set the speculation aside and spoke with Wiley-Gatewood. "We wanted to know what type of kid we were potentially getting," Frese said. "We wanted to know why she was leaving. I wanted to get to know her."

When Frese talked to the sophomore, she came away convinced Wiley-Gatewood was a good kid who would fit well into the team's fabric. Frese wanted her to meet the team and get its feedback, hence the invitation to the Christmas party and to the Duke game the following day. The visit to College Park went well for both Wiley-Gatewood and the Terps. After getting input from her team, Frese offered Wiley-Gatewood the opportunity to become a Terp.

Frese controls her players but allows them to play. She doesn't micromanage from the sideline, trusting her players' instincts instead. If the opportunity is there to push the ball or take an open shot, Frese expects her players to see it. After two years playing under the more rigid Summitt, it didn't take Wiley-Gatewood long to decide she wanted to spend the next 2 1/2 years in College Park.

"I went to a team gathering at Brenda's house, and the chemistry on this team is unbelievable," she said. "It's really different than Tennessee. We all got along, but there were different groups. On this team, there is just one big group."

While Wiley-Gatewood enjoyed her introduction to the team, the Terrapins turned their focus to the biggest game on the schedule — Duke.

The atmosphere was charged at the Comcast Center long before tip-off. Former Maryland football player LaMont Jordan, a longtime supporter of the program, was there. So were former Washington Redskins star Charles Mann and Kendel Ehrlich, wife of Maryland Gov. Robert Ehrlich, in anticipation of what they hoped would be a program-changing win.

Unfortunately, Maryland gave 16,097 fans, the second-largest crowd in ACC women's basketball history, little to cheer about in the first half. Duke, playing at its efficient best, was in control throughout, and a late run sent the Blue Devils into the half with a commanding 48-31 lead. The crowd was stunned, but no more so than the Terps, who were confident they were ready to beat Duke for the first time since 2000.

"You tell me, were we the most confident team out there in the first 20 minutes? Were we the hardest-working team out there in the first 20 minutes? Did we defend harder?" Frese scolded her team at the half. "Our team's M.O. has never been to hang our heads and think the game is over at halftime. Who said the game is over? We have way too much talent in this locker room to be acting like the game is over. Most teams when they come in at halftime with Duke they just fold and quit. What are you going to do?"

Maryland didn't quit, cutting the lead to nine on two occasions, but never really threatened the Blue Devils either, falling 86-68. Immediately following the game, Frese took the microphone, thanked the crowd for attending, and reminded the fans her team was "still something special" and would need their support.

With Toliver still not fully integrated back into the lineup after the shin injury — she played just 18 minutes — and Duke playing as well as any team in the country at the time, the loss shouldn't have been shocking. But the Terps desperately wanted to end Duke's dominance, and they weren't nearly as competitive as they expected to be. After the game, Frese didn't rip her players, opting instead to tell them the loss wasn't an altogether bad thing.

"We should thank Duke because Duke is going make us a better team come March," she said. "Big picture, this is just one game. They exposed a lot of things we need to get better at, but we showed a lot of character not folding."

Maryland didn't fold against the Blue Devils, but the game was a litmus test, and the results were eye-opening. Duke, which routed Tennessee by 20 points to take over the top spot in the polls 15 days later, dismantled the Terps in front of a fired-up Comcast Center crowd. The Blue Devils were determined to stop Langhorne and did. She finished with 10 points and, almost unbelievably, failed to grab a single rebound. She had never grabbed fewer than six rebounds in an ACC game to that point in her career. Duke shot 57.9 percent from the field and had its way with the Maryland defense.

The season wasn't even two full weeks into January, but Duke had already shown Maryland what a Final Four team looked like. The Terrapins had plenty of room to grow, but improvement was for the future. In the game's immediate aftermath, the bitterly disappointed team left the locker room and returned to the court to sign autographs for fans who hung around after the game.

The Terps had eight days off before their next game and needed the break. They had played five times in 11 days, and the Duke game was draining for everybody. Maryland returned to the court against a good Florida State team and showed no ill-effects, blowing out the Seminoles 75-57. The most encouraging part of the victory was Toliver's play. She came off the bench and scored a game-high 16 points in 27 minutes, the most she had played since the Tennessee game in November.

Maryland seemed to have put the Duke loss behind it and had, by ACC standards, a soft stretch of games in the coming weeks. The Terps had five games before a trip to North Carolina, and only one was against a NCAA Tournament team. First up was Virginia, and the once-powerful Cavaliers were having a down season. Maryland had won just three of the previous 25 games against Virginia and hadn't won in Charlottesville since January 1992, but that was expected to change.

The Cavaliers played as if they owned the Terps in the opening minutes, jumping out to a 15-6 lead. Maryland quickly countered with a run of its own, and momentum ebbed and flowed throughout the game. Virginia, in a trend the Terps would see often in the coming weeks, employed a smaller lineup, creating match-up problems in an attempt to neutralize Maryland's interior advantage. Frese countered by going to more of a four-guard lineup in the second half, playing Coleman, Doron, Newman and Toliver with Langhorne for long stretches.

The lineup was mostly effective, particularly Coleman, who scored a then-career-high 22 points, but the Terps were never able to gain any separation. Maryland had 23 turnovers and allowed the Cavaliers to shoot 53 percent from the field in the second half. With the score tied 67-67 in the waning seconds of regulation, Virginia had two shots to win the game but was unable to convert, forcing overtime. Relieved to have survived, Maryland took the drama out of the extra session with an early run and earned an 84-74 win. The Terps didn't play as well as they would have liked, but they earned another road win in a building that had been a house of horrors, so it was hard to be too disappointed.

Maryland's performance, particularly at the outset of games, didn't improve in the coming weeks. The Terps struggled at Virginia Tech, an NCAA Tournament team, getting bailed out when Toliver scored 10 straight points late in the game, to propel them to a 68-62 victory. Frese will chastise her players during games — all coaches do — but usually does so in a manner that ultimately reinforces her confidence in them. She may tell them they are playing poorly but without fail, Frese tells them they can correct their mistakes.

Like every coach, Frese's methods and approach to her team are shaped by her experiences in the game. Though there was no way of knowing it at the time, many of the decisions and events Frese endured as a player and young coach, helped prepare her to be a head coach. The first major decision she made — to leave home and go to Arizona — was also one of the most critical. Frese was wooed to Tucson by June Olkowski, a coach in her 20s with a relaxed approach to recruiting.

Unlike many coaches, Olkowski told jokes and was able to share a laugh with Frese, and the approach put Brenda at ease. Despite her pleasant demeanor on the recruiting trail, Olkowski's teams struggled on the court, and she was replaced after Frese's third year — a season she missed because of foot problems.

The transition to new coach Joan Bonvicini was instructive as well, particularly for someone who would be called upon to rebuild several programs in rapid succession. When a new coach arrives, there is nothing more uneasy than the relationship with the players, all of whom were recruited by the previous staff. Most coaching changes occur because of poor performance, and the new hire is brought in to change things. Those changes always have the greatest affect on the players, which creates anxiety. As a player, Frese experienced the awkward transition, made even more difficult for her because of the injury.

The most enduring lesson from Frese's days as a player and young coach was to try and stay as positive as possible with her players, a lesson hammered home when she coached her sister, Stacy, at Iowa State. Frese had the benefit of seeing the game through the eyes of a coach and a sister. The Cyclones were very successful when the Frese sisters were there — reaching the Elite Eight one year, knocking off UConn along the way — and Brenda gleaned invaluable experience from the situation.

"I learned through the course of the season that this wasn't a team that responded when they were getting down to more negativity, and most teams don't," Frese said. "It goes back to when I coached my sister and the insights she shared with me when she was a player. I don't think anyone on any stage goes out to compete and make mistakes. That doesn't have any logic to it. Everybody is going out there to succeed."

Frese works to build her players up, but still maintains the discipline necessary to run an effective team. "She does a nice job of being positive but intense," Bernabei said. "Even if she is getting in a girl's face yelling, she is saying, 'You are better than this,' as opposed to 'What the hell was that?' There are so many different ways to motivate girls, and she's picked the right one. There isn't a question of whether or not she has their backs. She cares for them. Yes, she is going to get on them and yell, but she spins it where it's a positive thing. You can be up in somebody's grill yelling but not degrading them. It's an intense 'You are better than this' type of demeanor as opposed to a 'You aren't going to be any good demeanor.' "

Despite her best efforts to remain positive, Frese reached her breaking point in the Virginia Tech game. Maryland trailed 27-24 at the half to a good Hokies team but not one that should have held the Terrapins down to the degree it did. For the first and really only time all season, Frese went after her players at the half. She questioned their heart, their motivation and reminded them in not so subtle fashion that, despite their No. 6 national ranking, they hadn't accomplished anything to date. Yes, the Terps were talented, but they weren't good enough to just show up and win. They had to respect their opponents and the challenge of playing on the road.

After Maryland survived the Hokies, Frese told the players she was glad they bounced back, but the team's play had to improve.

There was no immediate improvement. The Terps played a miserable first half at home against Georgia Tech the next time out, taking a narrow 34-30 lead into the break against a Yellow Jackets team that went 0-7 on the road in ACC play. Langhorne scored 19 of her 23 points in the second half to help the Terps pull away, but the victory did nothing to quell Frese's growing concern.

Maryland's saving grace rested in the fact that it was still winning games. The Terps' play was substandard and they had much to learn, but they were winning in the meantime. While the record continued to be sterling, players and coaches alike were searching for answers. A lack of intensity at the start of games seemed to be the biggest problem, allowing the opposition to build confidence and ensuring the Terps of a difficult night, particularly on the road.

The list of questions was long, and answers weren't easily forthcoming. Had the Terps, who nearly knocked off Tennessee in the Virgin Islands and seemed to have so much room to grow, played their best basketball of the season in November? It didn't seem possible, but they started to wonder.

"Sometimes when the coaches weren't around, we were like, 'What is wrong with us,' " Langhorne said. "It was kind of depressing. We'd be in the locker room and be like, 'We are too good to be playing like this.' "

The harder the Terps tried to figure out the problem, the more they struggled. On Jan. 29, Maryland stared down the most difficult moment of the season. The Terps traveled to Winston-Salem, N.C., for a Sunday afternoon game against Wake Forest. The Demon Deacons, who had lost at home to North Carolina by 34 points less than 48 hours earlier, seemingly had little chance. But nobody told Wake Forest it wasn't supposed to be competitive, and at the end of regulation the score was tied 64-64, forcing the Terps into their third overtime game in January. As baffling as the team's struggles were, another interesting trend continued: No matter how brutal Maryland's play was in regulation, it played well in overtime. Langhorne again stepped forward to lead the team, scoring 10 of her career-high 34 points in OT, and the Terps outscored Wake Forest 15-6 in the extra session to cruise to a 79-70 victory.

After the impressive showing in the Paradise Jam, Maryland had played without Toliver for much of December, and though she was playing a starter's minutes in January, she wasn't starting, which meant Doron and Coleman, to a lesser degree, were playing out of position.

On the trip home from Winston-Salem, a national championship wasn't on anybody's mind. The Terps needed to start improving in a hurry.

Chapter 8

"Boston '06"

Frese and Bernabei were eating dinner at a Cracker Barrel restaurant in West Virginia on their way to visit a prospective recruit in the fall of 2003. Cracker Barrel, a chain of restaurants famous for its country-style food, had never been a favorite of Frese's but Bernabei, a newcomer to the staff, lured her inside, and the meal proved much to the head coach's liking.

It was a crucial time for Frese entering her second summer at Maryland. The Terps were desperate for a talent upgrade, and the class of 2004 was one of the deepest and most talented in history. Frese signed her first class just months after accepting the job and landed an excellent crew, but with four scholarships to offer and a talented pool to recruit from, the class of 2004 was crucial in her efforts to rebuild the program.

Though Maryland experienced little success in the years before Frese's arrival and was coming off a 10-18 season, the young coach relentlessly pursued the nation's best players. With the new Comcast Center now opened, loads of local talent and a prime location between Washington, D.C. and Baltimore, Frese planned on turning the Terps into a national power. By her thinking, she wasn't going to accomplish it by accepting a place in the game's hierarchy based on her program's recent record. Frese went after the nation's top recruits and instead of running from Maryland's recent past, she embraced it.

Appealing to the confidence and pride inherent in any elite athlete, Frese pitched the idea of coming to Maryland to build a dynasty. Sure the players she was pursuing could go to UConn, Tennessee or Duke, but they would just be another in a long line of players and teams that achieved great success. Those were great programs, but particularly in the case of the Huskies and Lady Vols, a Final Four appearance and a national title would bring acclaim but not a prominent place in the program's history. Frese told recruits she was going to turn the Maryland program into a champion, and when the Terps won that first title, they would forever be a part of the program's lure, not names long forgotten among a horde of banners hanging from the arena ceiling.

Harper was one of the nation's more highly sought-after recruits, and Frese felt the Terps were positioned to land the emerging star. A gangly 6-4, Harper's first love was field hockey, but continued growth made it increasingly clear her future was on the hardwood. It took coordination and experience for Harper to catch up with her growing frame, but she emerged as one of the nation's top prospects with strong play on the AAU circuit.

Nearly every major program in the country coveted her. Her father, Haviland Harper, was a former basketball player at George Washington University, which kept the Colonials on the radar for quite some time before Harper eventually narrowed her choices to Maryland and UConn.

Frese and her staff worked diligently in their pursuit of Harper, starting long before her breakout performances at the summer Nike Camp. The Terps met with Harper's high school coach and used all five evaluation periods. They attended every AAU game possible and along the way developed an excellent, albeit high-maintenance, relationship with Harper. The Terps and UConn had each been to Harper's house for a visit and were preparing for a second when Maria Harper, Laura's mom, called in the middle of the meal at the Cracker Barrel.

Frese's jaw dropped when she heard what Maria Harper had to say: Laura had just verbally committed to UConn.

The decision blindsided Frese. Her initial reaction was that it was a joke because Laura Harper called often and enjoyed a good prank. The week before, Harper had told Frese Maryland was her likely choice, but she needed to discuss things with her parents. Harper even called Frese during an unofficial visit to UConn, making the news all the more stunning. Frese told Harper's mother she appreciated her time, and if Laura wanted to call and tell her of the decision personally she could do so anytime.

Frese felt as if she had been kicked in the stomach. Recruiting can be difficult to get a handle on. Highly coveted players are showered with attention from the most prominent names in women's basketball, and it's a difficult decision for a teenager. Unlike their classmates with college choices, prospective college athletes don't choose a school by returning the paperwork. Players have to call and tell a coach they have developed a relationship with that they don't want to spend the next four years with them. It's not easy.

Frese went from feeling good about the class she would be signing in the fall to wondering if it would unravel. Like anything else in athletics, there is a momentum to recruiting. When one top player commits, it is often easier for another to do so, and that was certainly true for a school in Maryland's situation. Frese felt a commitment from Harper could have had a domino effect on other prominent players.

The same night, Frese received a phone call from the upset Harper, who said her heart was at Maryland. Frese told Harper the day she chose her college should be among the happiest of her life. If Harper felt she made a mistake, it could be corrected, but the choice was hers alone. Harper told Frese she was going to sit down with her family and would be back in touch.

The family meeting was a good one for Harper. The recruiting process was overwhelming her. She was receiving text messages, calls from current players encouraging her to attend their schools, and word of the UConn commitment hit the news wires immediately. On top of the attention from players, coaches and even friends who assumed that anybody recruited by UConn would want to attend, Harper was now being besieged by the media.

"I was so overwhelmed I was crying," Harper said. "My mom was like, 'I don't want you dealing with this anymore.' I wanted to go to Maryland, and I made a decision I didn't want to. [The decision] wasn't binding and I could change [it]."

The Harpers told UConn they were reopening Laura's recruitment to Maryland and UConn within 48 hours of her verbal, but Maria laid out a different set of ground rules for both schools. The recruitment of Laura Harper, one of the top three centers in her class and the 14th-ranked prospect overall, went from crazy to quiet nearly overnight. Each school could make one weekly call on the Harper's landline, nothing else, and Laura quit burning the free minutes on her cell phone with outgoing calls. Each school was allowed a second in-home visit, but Harper would make her final decision in relative peace.

When the uproar surrounding her commitment and then de-commitment to UConn subsided, it became easier for Harper to make the decision she felt was the right one all along. In the early part of October, about a month before signing day, Harper committed to Maryland.

"Coach B's passion and her dream sold me," Harper said. "I wanted to go somewhere I was going to be happy. You have to spend your waking hours with these people, and you have to feel like it's going to be OK. She's a head coach that is always there, and I can't say that about any other coach that recruited me. It wasn't like she threw some assistants on me [to handle a lot of the recruiting]. She cared. She had me believing I was going to be a big piece of the puzzle, and you really can't turn something like that down. She kind of challenged me: 'Do you really want to take this team to a championship? We need you here, and we are going to win.' Her confidence really made me want to come here."

Harper's commitment to Maryland opened Frese to charges of recruiting a player who verbally committed elsewhere, an assertion she categorically denied.

"There was some misinformation people put out there that we had recruited her after she verbaled, but that wasn't the case," Frese said. "Anytime a kid verbals to another school, we don't recruit them. She contacted us and said she had made a mistake and wanted to go back and open it back up."

Stunning as it may have been to some, Frese had taken on the three-time defending national champion Connecticut Huskies on the recruiting trail and beaten them. It was the highest-profile recruiting battle the Terps had won to date but wasn't the last — though Frese had eaten her last meal at a Cracker Barrel.

If Harper's recruitment provided more than enough drama, the pursuit of her classmate, Langhorne, couldn't have been more different. The top post player in the class of 2004 and the eighth-ranked prospect overall, Langhorne didn't require a lot of attention. She was a throwback to a different era in terms of how she was recruited. The Internet had changed recruiting. The NCAA restricts the number of phone calls prospective recruits can receive from schools, but there are no limitations on e-mail, instant messaging and text messaging, the preferred form of communication for many prospects.

Langhorne eschewed modern technology when it came to her recruitment. She didn't e-mail, instant message or text message coaches, much less call them. Communication was limited to the NCAA's allowable one phone call a week and conventional mail. While Frese often develops a pretty good feel for where Maryland stands with recruits, the process was much more difficult with Langhorne, who wasn't shy but didn't talk just to hear herself. She answered questions and engaged in conversation but didn't reveal any leanings.

Frese knew two things about Langhorne: Every time she narrowed her list, the Terps made the cut, and she was a young woman of tremendous character. Langhorne really listened to what Frese was saying and read the letters she was sent. Frese once sent Langhorne — who, like most recruits in the East, told her she didn't know much about Iowa — an article on ice cream in the Hawkeye state. The next time they talked, Langhorne laughed about an aspect of the story. The article was a minor part of a recruitment that unfolded over more than a year, but Frese felt it revealing about Langhorne. The young star might not have had much to say, but she was a sponge, absorbing everything she read, saw and heard.

The one thing that wasn't going to work with Langhorne was pressure. The recruiting process is different for everyone, but Langhorne had at least some experience with it because her two older brothers had played low-level Division I basketball. Cryhten Langhorne was a four-year letter-winner at the University of Maryland-Eastern Shore and Chris Langhorne was a player at Texas State. "Recruiting didn't bother me at all," Langhorne said. "I don't like to get stressed so I was just real relaxed. I wasn't going to let anybody pressure me."

There was no pressure on Langhorne, but the coaches pursuing her were anything but relaxed. Langhorne, who took official visits to Florida, UConn, Maryland and Virginia, narrowed her list to the Terps and Huskies. At that point, the decision became tough. "Recruiting was real easy for me until my last decision," she said. "It was a big decision because Maryland wasn't very good and people were like, 'Go to UConn.'"

On the evening Langhorne was making her decision, Frese sat nervously in her townhouse. She was a program-changing player, along with Harper, and Frese knew her commitment could make Maryland a national force. She challenged Langhorne to help her build a champion, just as she had Harper, and Langhorne soothed Frese's nerves with a commitment to Maryland.

"A lot of people said, 'You are foolish — I can't believe you are going to Maryland,'" Langhorne said. "But [Frese] rebuilt Minnesota and she already had Shay and Kalika. At other schools, the assistant coaches called more. At Maryland, I talked to Coach B more. Coach B played a big part, and I think that really helped her out."

The commitments and eventual signings of Harper and Langhorne

Maryland Coach Brenda Frese, addressing the crowd at Maryland Madness, worked tirelessly to raise awareness of her team.

The relationship between Brenda Frese and point guard Kristi Toliver grew throughout the course of the season.

Following their run to the national championship, the Terrapins made a 12-day, four-game tour of Europe that included a visit to the Eiffel Tower in Paris, France.

Debbie Yow and Brenda Frese saw the potential for greatness in the Maryland women's basketball program.

The Terps answer questions for a throng of reporters at the Final Four in Boston.

Maryland assistant coach Erica Floyd and NFL standout LaMont Jordan, a Maryland alum and avid fan of the team, pose after the national championship game.

Laura Harper developed from a sophomore not sure of her role on the team to the Most Outstanding Player in the Final Four.

Crystal Langhorne (center), Ashleigh Newman (left) and Marissa Coleman begin celebrating the first national championship in program history.

Crystal Langhorne presents President George W. Bush with a Maryland jersey in a ceremony at the White House honoring the Terps.

Brenda Frese and her husband Mark Thomas took a limo ride to the ESPYs after Maryland was nominated for Best Team in 2006 at the network's annual event in Los Angeles.

The Frese family, gathered at the Final Four, is (left to right) sister-in-law Christy, sister Marsha, mother Donna, brother Jeff, sister Stacy, father Bill, sister Cindy and nephew Jordan.

established that Frese would make the Terps a significant player on the national scene sooner rather than later. Some observers, accustomed to the nation's top recruits flocking to traditional powers, were stunned Maryland landed its class — though that line of thinking was rooted in arrogance and an assumption that young women weren't capable of seeing beyond the expectations of others.

"That is one thing that separates men's and women's basketball. You see a lot of men's players going to random schools — the best players go everywhere," Langhorne said. "We want more parity in the game, and I think us coming [to Maryland] is helping people see they don't have to go to UConn or Tennessee."

The attention surrounding the 2004 recruiting class focused on Harper and Langhorne, but the signings of Perry and Newman spoke just as highly of Frese's recruiting ability. She went into the South, customarily not a recruiting hotbed for the Terps, and landed two prized prospects who were being heavily courted. Perry, a native of Central City, Ky., is generously listed at 6-1, but she is the team's strongest player and rugged post defender. She was dominant on both ends of the floor at Muhlenberg North High School, finishing her career with 2,792 points, 1,647 rebounds and 512 blocks but wasn't regarded as an elite recruit.

Perry's talent didn't elude the Terps' coaching staff. Marsha Frese and Walz believed Perry could give Maryland needed strength in the middle. The challenge was to lure her out of Kentucky. Louisville, Western Kentucky and Kentucky were pursuing her, and most assumed she would stay in-state, with Western Kentucky, whose campus was less than an hour from her house, her likeliest destination. Central City had six stoplights and less than 6,000 residents — a subject that remains a source of amusement to Perry's current teammates — and she had wanted to play for Western Kentucky growing up. While the Hilltoppers don't resonate with many Maryland fans, they have a tradition of success in the women's game, including a pair of Final Four appearances in the 1990s. The idea that an all-state selection would want to attend Western Kentucky is anything but farfetched in the Bluegrass State, but after one trip to College Park for Maryland's Elite Individual Camp, Perry was ready to pack her bags and head to Maryland for good.

"I just fell in love with the program," Perry said in her heavy Southern drawl. "I came up here on an unofficial visit, and the campus was just so beautiful. Before I was even thinking about Maryland, I was going to go to Western Kentucky. I came back from my visit and told my mama I was ready to verbal, but she wouldn't let me until she saw it first. I believed in Coach B and the program, and I wanted to come make a difference."

Perry visited with her mother in August before her senior year and shortly thereafter pledged her commitment.

While Perry came to Maryland from a small town without a tradition of churning out high-major Division I basketball players, Newman hailed from a virtual basketball factory in Murfreesboro, Tenn., just outside Nashville. She helped lead Shelbyville Central High School to state championships as a junior and senior, earning tournament most valuable player honors both years. Shelbyville was coached at the time by Rick Insell, who later accepted the head coaching job at Middle Tennessee State in 2005, and his players were coveted by college coaches. Insell ran a no-nonsense program, demanding excellence on the court and in the classroom. Shelbyville sent 57 players into the college ranks during Insell's tenure, and his players were as prepared as any for the adjustment to Division I hoops.

Newman grew up in a state that holds women's basketball in higher regard than any other and was an all-state selection and team MVP for a state champion. The people predicting Newman was going to head north to College Park didn't extend beyond the Maryland coaching staff and possibly their immediate families. The doubters included Newman herself.

Although Newman grew up as a Tennessee fan, the Lady Vols were never significant competitors for her; Alabama, Kentucky and, to a lesser degree, Georgia, were. Newman received correspondence from Maryland, but her initial interest was non-existent. When her family made a summer trip to see relatives in Fort Washington, Md., Newman's mom called the women's basketball office and asked if they could come by for an unofficial visit, a development that didn't please her daughter. "To be honest, I didn't want to go," Newman said. "I didn't want to go to Maryland, so why would I want to take a visit?"

One forced unofficial visit later, however, the sharp-shooting Newman was hooked. By the time she took her official visit as a senior, it was all over but the signing.

On Nov. 12, 2003, Harper, Langhorne, Newman and Perry signed national letters of intent with Maryland, providing a boost to Frese's rebuilding job not even the most optimistic of Terps fans could have dreamed of just two years before.

Marissa Coleman and Kristi Toliver, in town for the McDonald's and Women's Basketball Coaches Association All-American games, sat in the RCA Dome in Indianapolis in the spring of 2005 watching the women's Final Four and vowed to be playing in the event a year later. Youthful naivete? Yes. But there was no denying the talent and just as important, the moxie, the rising freshmen would bring to Maryland in the fall. With Doron and France returning and the heralded class of 2004 promising better days, Frese and the Terps knew they were on the verge of something special.

The one component the Terps lacked was a point guard, but the staff felt it had found one in Toliver. A multi-talented player from Harrisonburg, Va., the quiet location of James Madison University, Toliver had burst onto the recruiting scene the summer before her senior year. She didn't play the AAU circuit as much as some of her contemporaries, but that didn't diminish her talent or Maryland's interest. Toliver was coveted by Virginia and Virginia Tech, each an easy drive from her home. But the Cavaliers, once a perennial women's power, were struggling, and Hokies coach Bonnie Henrickson had left for Kansas, leaving the door open for Maryland and UConn, Toliver's favorite team.

When Bernabei made her first trip to Toliver's home, she was greeted by an assortment of UConn basketball posters. Swin Cash, Sue Bird and Taurasi adorned Toliver's walls, but instead of being bothered by UConn's presence, Bernabei and the Terps used it to their advantage. There wouldn't be another Bird, Taurasi or Cash at UConn, but Toliver could be the Terrapins' equivalent if she chose to come to College Park.

"Did I ever think I'd be at Maryland at that point? No," Toliver said. "But what I saw at Maryland was [being] that UConn team. That's what I talked to Coach B about. We had the same vision and saw the same things."

The Terps also had another powerful incentive to offer Toliver: immediate playing time. The talent Frese had assembled was obvious, but the graduation of Smith was going to leave a hole in the lineup for which there was no natural successor. Frese told Toliver the Terps were on their way to a title and the team was hers to lead, an invitation she couldn't resist.

Long before Toliver and Coleman sat in Indianapolis plotting their trip to the Final Four, they became friends on the AAU circuit and in their recruiting travels. In many ways, the two couldn't be more different. Coleman has a body that looks as if it were built for the game, she has an outgoing personality and she is one of the team clowns. Toliver could be the girl next door and chooses her words carefully, but talent drew them together. They met while both were being recruited by West Virginia — a move that bit the Mountaineers "in the butt," Coleman says with a laugh — and hit it off. Toliver came to spend Memorial Day weekend 2004 with the Coleman family at their Cheltenham, Md., home, and they were joined by Harper, who already had signed a letter of intent to attend Maryland. The trio called Frese and asked if she would be around for their visit.

Frese and her staff rearranged their Memorial Day weekend schedule to accommodate the highly regarded trio thinking this was just another visit — none of the three players was unfamiliar with campus — but Coleman and Toliver had other plans. After spending Saturday at the Comcast Center, Coleman and Toliver returned on Sunday and informed Frese they had something to tell her.

They both wanted to commit to the University of Maryland. In fact, Toliver called UConn coach Geno Auriemma and canceled an unofficial visit planned for the next weekend.

Frese was ecstatic. In the course of six months, the Terps had signed the No. 2-ranked recruiting class in the nation, advanced to the second round of the NCAA Tournament and secured verbal commitments from two of the top players in the class of 2005. Less than 2 1/2 years after her arrival, Frese had enough talent signed and was seemingly on her way to contend for the national title she came to Maryland to win.

Coleman's mother was waiting outside, and they brought her in to celebrate. Toliver's parents were concerned that Kristi had gotten caught up in the moment while having a good time with Harper, a signee, and Coleman, a good friend. She assured them that wasn't the case, and Maryland was the place where she wanted to spend her college years.

Toliver never wavered in her commitment, but the battle for Coleman was just beginning. Coleman's father, Tony, was also her AAU coach, and she had been playing the summer circuit for years. Her talent wasn't a secret to any coach in the country or USA Basketball. As a rising senior in high school, she made the USA U19 team and spent a portion of the summer practicing for and playing in the Junior World Championship Qualifying Tournament in Mayaguez, Puerto Rico. One of the assistants with the team was Florida coach Carolyn Peck, with whom Coleman grew close during the weeks the team spent playing together. The squad went 5-0 and won the gold medal.

Once the U19 team completed its tournament and returned to the United States, Coleman reopened her recruitment after enjoying time with Peck. At some level, Frese may have understood Coleman's confusion, but it didn't make it any less frustrating. Coleman had been around the Maryland campus more than any recruit in Frese's tenure. She lived just miles down the road and had been attending games for years. She knew her future teammates well — Harper was a teammate on the U19 team that played in Puerto Rico — and got along well with them.

When Coleman committed, Frese stopped recruiting other guards in the class of 2005. It would have been difficult to replace a player of Coleman's talent with a year's notice, much less the three months between her de-commitment and signing day. But Coleman was important for more than just her talent. She was a local kid and, most importantly to Frese and her staff, a good kid. They wanted players and people like Coleman. But Frese is a realist, and history told her that players who rescind a commitment usually don't come back. Coleman knew everything there was to know about the Terps program — there was nothing else Frese could tell or show her — and still she had second thoughts.

Despite her concern, Frese continued to recruit Coleman as much as allowed, but it was an awkward time. Frese made the allowed visit to St. John's College High School in nearby Washington, D.C., where Coleman attended, in September. Coleman still swayed between the two schools, made an official visit to Florida and wanted to make one to Maryland, but Frese, who doesn't pressure prospects to commit, had a caveat. She would welcome Coleman for an official visit only to celebrate her re-commitment. She reinforced to Coleman that she knew everything there was to know about the program and the people in it, and there was nothing further she would learn on an "official" visit.

With a suitable replacement nowhere to be found, the Terps waited for Coleman's decision. Maryland was going to be talented whether Coleman committed or not. But Coleman, like several other players on the team, was a difference maker. She was a first-team Parade All-American, a first-team All USA Basketball team member as named by USA Today, and the Washington Post's high school player of the year as a senior. Players of Coleman's ilk were the difference between very good and great teams.

Heartbreak struck the Terrapins' staff that fall as Bernabei's father died, unbeknownst to Coleman. As Frese left the funeral service in West

Virginia, she checked the messages on her cell phone. Coleman had called and re-committed.

"It was crazy," Coleman said of her recruitment. "I came very close to going to Florida, but after looking at the pros and cons, I couldn't see myself anywhere other than Maryland. My teammates, my coaches and being close to home — it was a better fit for me here."

As for Toliver, she had doubts about her friend's destination but didn't try to force her hand.

"She was like, 'Were you going to take that trip up to UConn if I hadn't verbaled with you?' " Toliver said of Coleman telling her about Florida reentering the picture. "I was like, 'Why are you asking me this, Marissa?' She said, 'I think I'm going to take a trip to Florida.' I was a little worried at one point, but I had a feeling she would be here. I never told her 'You can't do that,' but she knew I would be a little disappointed."

After Coleman renewed her commitment to Maryland and signed a letter of intent a month later, her focus returned to the pact she had made with Toliver. Coleman's away-message on her instant message account made her ambitions perfectly clear. It said, simply, "Boston '06."

Yet the recruit who had ignited the Terps' return to prominence was Doron. When Frese accepted the Maryland job, she wasted little time targeting Doron, a top 10 guard. Frese built her reputation as a persuasive recruiter over time, but she had very little of that on her side when she pursued Doron. The factor she did have in her favor was Doron's love of a challenge. As smart as she was gifted, Doron seriously considered Stanford and Harvard before eventually becoming the first vital cog in Frese's rebuilding project at Maryland.

"She is persuasive as a recruiter, but she doesn't need to do much," Doron said. "She is like, 'This is what I'm about, this is what I think you are about and this is what we can do together. Are you willing to take that chance with me?' She never told me I was going to come in and be a superstar or we aren't ever going to lose. She wasn't promising you everything, and that's what I loved. Everybody was real. They told me everything I should expect academically and basketball-wise."

After Doron committed, Frese and Walz visited her New York home for what amounted to a celebration. After eating kosher food for the first time, Frese and Walz left the official visit hungry but happy. Signing a player of Doron's caliber merely whet their appetite for recruiting.

Chapter 9

Assistant Coaches

After Frese's first interview with Maryland, she wanted College Park to be her next coaching stop. She was dazzled by the Comcast Center, still under construction, and the school, which was perfectly situated between Baltimore and Washington, D.C. and a manageable drive from Philadelphia and New York, some of the game's most fertile recruiting grounds.

When Frese returned to Minneapolis after the one-day interview, she immediately called her Minnesota staff members to see if they were available to meet that night at Pearson's apartment. Frese and her staff had experienced tremendous success in their one season at Minnesota and had grown close along the way. Everybody on the staff had a different personality, but basketball and small town upbringings — Midwestern sensibilities, if you will — were the common bonds between them.

The Minnesota staff was available for the night meeting, and Frese excitedly relayed what she had seen at Maryland and the possibilities she envisioned. If she were offered the job, would they come with her?

On the outside, Minnesota looked like a dream scenario: Young coach and young staff turn around floundering program and become media and fan darlings. Appearances can be misleading, though. On the court, Brenda and Marsha Frese, Walz and Floyd were happy, but they spent only a small portion of their day there. The separate men's and women's athletic departments were a nuisance at best and a serious competitive drag at worst. With separate logos, facilities and department staffs, there was a feeling of competition as opposed to camaraderie. Frustrated by the off-court machinations at Minnesota, which has since merged the two athletic departments, the staff knew if the right opportunity arose, moving for the second time in a year was a real possibility.

Though nobody on the staff had ever lived on the East Coast, the assistants all agreed to move to Maryland if necessary. Walz and Floyd were onboard immediately. It was a little tougher for Marsha, whose husband was from Minnesota and Pearson, who had an infant son and, along with his wife, was from the Midwest, but both quickly decided College Park would be their next home.

Walz is the coaching version of a gym rat. There is no such thing as too much tape to watch, practices that run too long or a game that doesn't need to be analyzed. He loves the competition of game day and the process leading up to it. Walz relishes the challenge of preparing for an unfamiliar opponent and devising a game plan that leaves the opposition shaking its collective head.

Walz grew up in Fort Thomas, a small town just inside the Kentucky line and 20 miles from Cincinnati. Family and sports were the two primary factors in Walz's life. His father Roger was a teacher and football coach in the Fort Thomas school system for 30 years. If Roger wasn't coaching a game, Jeff, his two older brothers or his younger sister were playing in one. In fact, Walz's family is directly responsible for him being a women's college coach.

After a standout playing career at Highlands High School in Fort Thomas, Walz was on the team for two years at Northern Kentucky University, but his playing career had run its course. With nothing more than pickup games on his agenda, Walz, on a whim, asked his sister Jaime if she would be interested in playing for an AAU team if he started one. Jaime was a highly regarded prep player — she was named 1996 National High School Player of the Year — and was more than pleased to play for her brother.

Lacking the urban areas that have scads of Division I prospects to pack AAU teams, many Kentucky prospects went across the state line to play summer ball with Cincinnati teams. The Bluegrass State isn't a recruiting hotbed for women's basketball, but it had several elite prospects cycling through with Jaime Walz. With his sister on board, Walz persuaded several of the state's other top prospects to join his team, including Ukari Figgs, who went on to win NCAA and WNBA titles; Kyra Elzy, who went to Tennessee; and future Ohio State standout Marita Porter. The Kentucky Hustle was born that quickly.

Walz's older brother, Scott, helped coach the team, and the Hustle lived up to its nickname, soliciting help from the community to fund trips. The team raised its own travel money, practiced a couple of days before tournaments and enjoyed great success, finishing third in an AAU national tournament in Cleveland. Jaime Walz caught the eye of recruiters from across the country, but she opted to stay home and attend Western Kentucky while the Kentucky Hustle ceased to exist after Jaime graduated from high school. Jeff's work with the Hustle caught the attention of Western Kentucky coach Paul Sanderford, one of the game's best. Sanderford offered Walz, who had just graduated from Northern Kentucky with a degree in secondary education, a job as a graduate assistant. In the state of Kentucky, a master's degree is required for a long-term teaching career, so the decision was easy for Walz.

After Walz's second year at Western Kentucky, Sanderford, who had led the Hilltoppers to 12 NCAA Tournament and three Final Four appearances in 15 years, accepted the head job at Nebraska and invited his staff to join him in Lincoln. Walz, who had always planned to coach and teach in the public school system, had his career path changed. Though he was an assistant at Western Kentucky, the crux of Walz's coaching education took place at Nebraska. Unencumbered by graduate school, Walz immersed himself in coaching. From coaching to recruiting, he was involved in all aspects of the game.

His travels on the recruiting trail brought him into contact with Frese, a young Iowa State assistant at the time, and a mutual respect grew out of those meetings as well as the hardwood battles between Iowa State and Nebraska, who were NCAA Tournament regulars at the time. When Frese moved from Ball State to Minnesota, she had the type of job opening that enticed Walz. After he called to congratulate Frese on landing the job, talk quickly turned to her staff, and Walz was an obvious choice. He talked with Sanderford, who highly recommended the move as being in Walz's long-term best interest, and accepted the job shortly thereafter.

The working relationship between Walz and Frese was excellent from the start, and he quickly grew into her most trusted on-court lieutenant. Walz is not a "yes man," and Frese has always been secure enough to listen to what other people say. If Frese and Walz differ in opinion, the final decision is ultimately hers, but neither holds a grudge. As Frese puts it, he isn't afraid to "challenge my way of thinking."

Walz loves the intricacies of the game, such as teaching during practice and diagramming plays, and is very good at it. His tactical proficiency allows Frese to recruit on non-game days knowing her team won't miss a beat in practices. In recent years as a game neared a media time-out or Frese sensed the need for a big offensive set, she looked to Walz, while she directed in game action, and had him plot a play for the team when it emerged from the timeout. With only 30 seconds allotted for timeouts, Frese trusts Walz to create several options in advance to avoid a hurried decision at a critical point. Their relationship would pay huge dividends in the NCAA Tournament.

Frese and Floyd were recent college graduates not ready to give up the game they loved despite the end of their respective playing careers. The desire to stay in the game led both to start their coaching career at Kent State. Frese was hired as the third assistant on Coach Lindsay's staff in 1993 and moved up a spot the following season, making room for Floyd on the staff. Though they were together for just one season — Frese left for Iowa State in 1995 — the pair hit it off from the start. Both had come from tightly knit families in the Midwest — Floyd was from Kent, a town of fewer than 30,000 located about 20 miles from Akron — and they had much in common.

As two young people working to make it in a hyper-competitive field, they developed a close friendship through their shared experience. After Frese left, they kept in touch, exchanging birthday cards, making occasional phone calls and attempting to meet up on the summer recruiting circuit. When Frese became head coach at Minnesota, she invited Floyd to join her staff, and she jumped from Cleveland State to Minnesota and the Big Ten. Even after Floyd agreed to make the move, she had second thoughts late in the process, at least in part because she had never lived outside Ohio.

The move worked out well for both. They have remained good friends, and Floyd is an invaluable part of Frese's staff. Aside from being a vital cog in the Terps' recruiting machinery, Floyd is the staff's "glue" person, in large part because she is a good listener. Whether it's a player having a problem or a coach having a bad day, Floyd is someone every player and staff member trusts. She doesn't take sides and keeps things in confidence.

One of the primary reasons Floyd sought out a career as a coach was a less-than-optimal experience during her playing days. "I didn't really have a great experience," Floyd said. "I didn't have a really good relationship with my head coach. We only spoke because we had to. I wanted to get into coaching to see if that's how it had to be. Is that how it is in every program?"

Shaped by those experiences, Floyd, who by her own admission didn't feel as if she were completely part of the team during her senior season at Ohio State, works to make sure everyone stays involved. With an easy laugh and an engaging smile, Floyd puts everybody at ease, a beneficial trait on the recruiting trail and within the team.

On the court, her work with Maryland's post players has clearly been effective. Langhorne, Harper and Perry have shown tremendous improvement in their two years at College Park, and their work with Floyd, a 6-3 post player in her playing days, is one of the primary reasons. While her size made the basketball court a natural destination, it wasn't necessarily the sport in which she enjoyed the most success. Floyd was a track standout at Theodore Roosevelt High School in Kent, winning state championships in the 200-meter dash and 4 x 400 relay as a senior.

Marsha Frese joined her sister in College Park for a year, playing a vital role in the recruitment of a class ranked 10th in the nation. Marsha, like her sister, is a rising star in the profession, but in her quest to become a head coach, she thought it was in her best interest to have someone other than her sister on her list of references. After the 2002-03 season, she was hired at Illinois, creating a vacancy on the Maryland staff.

Brenda Frese, who keeps her eyes open for rising young assistants, quickly moved to add Bernabei, West Virginia's recruiting coordinator, to her staff. Much like she had with Walz, Frese met Bernabei on the recruiting trail, where the latter's energy level and personality stood out. A standout point guard at West Liberty State College in West Virginia, Bernabei was a perfect fit for Maryland. She was young — 28 at the time of her hiring — confident and had a track record that would make a coach 10 years her senior proud.

After finishing her playing career as one of the few players in NCAA history with more than 1,000 points and 1,000 assists (she holds the NCAA Division II assists record with 1,107), Bernabei earned her master's degree at Eastern Kentucky, where she worked as an assistant coach during the 1997-98 season. Her gritty play left an impression throughout the West Virginia Intercollegiate Athletic Conference, where she was a four-year, first team all-conference performer, and she was hired as head coach and senior women's administrator at West Virginia Wesleyan College in 1998 at age 23. Bernabei excelled, leading Wesleyan to an 18-9 record and a third place finish in the WVIAC, an extremely competitive D-II league. Though she enjoyed being quite possibly the youngest head coach in NCAA history — Summitt became a coach at 22, but women's basketball was governed by the AIAW at the time — a full-time assistant's position opened up at Eastern Kentucky, and she jumped at the opportunity.

Bernabei, who had never recruited a D-I athlete, became Eastern Kentucky's recruiting coordinator in 1999, and her performance put her on the fast track. In addition to recruiting, Bernabei was in charge of scheduling, and she tried to call Ball State and a young coach named Frese every day for three weeks about scheduling a game. It didn't happen, but that was one of her few failures. Bernabei, with virtually no files, was told to start recruiting. She created a database and went to work for coach Larry Joe Inman.

Bernabei has always trusted her instincts in evaluating talent, and they have served her well. In her first summer as the Colonels' recruiting coordinator, she was scouting a tournament at Robert Morris College in Pittsburgh, just miles from her hometown in Weirton, W.Va., when an undersized point guard caught her eye. Katie Kelly, who had a late growth spurt — she was barely 5 feet tall as a sophomore in high school — wasn't being recruited by anyone, even tournament host Robert Morris, which was one of the worst teams in the nation at the time.

Bernabei looked at the baby-faced Kelly and saw something apparently no other Division I coach did. Eastern Kentucky signed Kelly, who eventually grew to 5-6, without much of a fight, though Inman didn't see her playing much as a slightly built freshman. In the Colonels' first game of the season against Texas A&M, the starting point guard picked up two early fouls, forcing Kelly onto the court. She responded with an excellent effort and never left the starting lineup. Kelly finished her career fourth on the school's all-time scoring list and second in assists.

That type of recruiting effort and an old WVIAC connection led the fiery Bernabei to West Virginia, where she was recruiting coordinator and helped turn a struggling program into a NCAA Tournament team. Mike Carey, who was men's coach at Salem College, a WVIAC member, was hired at West Virginia, and Bernabei jokes that she got the job because she was the only female coach he knew. Bernabei was planning to apply for a head coach's job until Frese called. She toured the

Maryland campus and decided that working for Frese, her first female boss, was a good career move.

Thankfully for Bernabei, the coaching thing has worked out well. She has loved the game as long as she can remember. With her siblings, two sisters and a brother, between eight and 10 years older than she is, Bernabei spent a lot of time as a team mascot before playing organized basketball — occasionally in boys' leagues — beginning at age 6. A professed basketball junkie, Bernabei later coached a fifth-grade team and an all-star squad of 12-year-olds. While her passion for the game was apparent to everyone, her post-college life also seemed to have a clear direction: She was going to attend pharmacy school and work as a pharmacist with her older brother.

As Bernabei prepared for the WVIAC tournament during her senior year, the West Virginia Pharmacy School, where her brother sat on the board, was expecting an application that never arrived. The only problem was, Bernabei hadn't told anyone in her family she wasn't ready to give up basketball. At the conference tournament, Bernabei's mother asked her about the pharmacy school application — she had been taking preparatory classes — when she told her mother she had made alternate career plans. "I told my mom, 'I'm not going,' and she said, 'You have to,' " Bernabei recalled. "I said, 'Maybe in a couple of years.' I just couldn't imagine not having basketball as part of my life."

Bernabei finally earned her family's forgiveness, and her alternate career path has worked out well.

Chapter 10

*First Family of Cedar
Rapids Athletics*

W ashington High School in Cedar Rapids, Iowa, was throwing a pep rally to send its girls' basketball team into the 1988 state tournament. A local radio station was broadcasting live, and the band was playing. The Warriors would be facing national power Waterloo Columbus, ranked No. 1 in the state and No. 3 in the nation, according to USA Today, and one of the few people who expected the Warriors to win was their team captain. Brenda Frese, a gangly senior who averaged 26.6 points, had no intention of ending her high school career with a loss, and she told her assembled classmates as much. "We aren't just going to play in the state tournament," she told them. "We are going to win it."

Frese made 11 of 20 shots and scored 22 points to lead the Warriors to a stunning 64-59 win at Veterans Auditorium in Des Moines. In the state title game, she capped her prep career with a brilliant 35-point, 13-rebound, 4-steal performance in a 65-47 win over Bettendorf.

The traits that define Frese as a coach in her mid-30s are no different than they were when she was one of six siblings growing up in Cedar Rapids. She was competitive, fearless and worked hard in pursuit of her goals.

Athletic excellence and competition were common denominators for Bill and Donna Frese's children. Beginning with Jeff, the only son, the family established something of an athletic dynasty in Cedar Rapids, sending four kids on to play Division I sports. Bill and Donna never forced their kids to play, but they were enormously supportive, toting them to practices and games and working with them for hours in the backyard. Bill built a batting cage in the backyard for Jeff, who played baseball at Northern Iowa.

Jeff started the Frese family's athletic run, but his three younger sisters were the ones who made the family name familiar to local basketball fans. Until the 1984-85 school year, girls in Iowa played 6-on-6 basketball, which fit Brenda's game perfectly — she played offense with abandon and got to stop at halfcourt and let someone else take over on the defensive end. From the moment Frese started playing the game, she fell in love with it.

She spent hours outside shooting and when the cold Iowa winters descended, Bill had the key to a local gym and would go rebound for her until she was tired of shooting. Marsha was just two years younger, and the two siblings were competitive in every aspect of their lives, even to the point of seeing who could shoot longer. The competitiveness led to a few contentious evenings in the Frese home, but both were working to improve.

Nothing stopped the Frese girls from playing basketball, including a couple of black eyes. Once at a family gathering, Brenda, in the ninth grade, took an elbow between the eyes from her godfather in a pickup game that left her with both eyes blackened, but she soldiered on.

Like her older siblings, Brenda attended a private Catholic school, Regis, but as 6-on-6 gave way to the contemporary full-court game, Frese wanted the opportunity to improve, and that meant public schools. She convinced her parents to send her to Washington, where she had the opportunity to play for Paul James during a golden era for girls' high school basketball in Iowa. The decision to transfer as a sophomore wasn't easy, but Frese immediately took to public school. She was exposed to greater diversity than she had known at Regis, and the level of competition rose.

Frese spent her summer months playing AAU basketball. In 1985, Bill bought a new white van to haul his kids to tournaments, including one trip that is still vividly recalled by Brenda and Marsha. Just after their father purchased the van, the Freses trekked to Clovis, N.M., for a tournament and drove through a freshly tarred section of road. The lower third of the shiny, white van was covered in tar, small rocks and other debris by the time they arrived in Clovis. A stray rock even cracked the windshield, leading to a less than pleasant evening. "Dad was obsessed with keeping that van clean," Marsha recalled with a laugh. "We probably spent three hours cleaning the bottom of that thing."

The trip to Clovis was like many others the family experienced over the summer — they took one route to the tournament and another on the way back, building a vacation around the basketball tournament. After the event in Clovis, they went to California for a trip to Disneyland, but basketball was still foremost in their minds. Each of the girls brought her own ball, and Bill typically found a local school so they could shoot after visiting Mickey Mouse. By this time, the youngest and arguably the most gifted sister, Stacy, also was tagging along, so there was no shortage of bouncing balls at the Frese house.

Like Brenda, Marsha transferred to Washington High as a sophomore, and the two sisters were teammates during the school's 1988 state title run. Stacy ended the Frese's era as the first family of Cedar Rapids athletics when she led Washington to the 1995 state title. Marsha accepted a scholarship to play at Rice University. Stacy started at Iowa before transferring to Iowa State, where Brenda was on staff with the Cyclones.

With her success on the AAU circuit and at Washington High, Brenda had several colleges pursuing her and chose Arizona. But Tucson was more than 1,700 miles from Cedar Rapids, and the distance was difficult for her and her family.

The week before Brenda left home, Bill and Donna took Stacy to a tournament in Puerto Rico, and Brenda spent her last week in Cedar Rapids dealing with her fears of flying to Arizona by herself. The person who was supposed to pick her up in Tucson, teammate Julie Mendivil, got lost on the way to the airport and was 45 minutes late. Frese stood in the airport without a calling card wondering what she was going to do. Mendivil, who remains a close friend, eventually arrived, but Frese's transition to Tucson was difficult.

She struggled to make the adjustment to playing against bigger, faster competition, and she was lost in the weight room, though none of it compared to her homesickness. She played off the bench during her freshman year, and Olkowski felt she had a bright future, but Frese stunned her coach when she asked to be released from her scholarship so she could transfer closer to home.

Olkowski didn't overreact to Frese's request and instead took her outside where the two calmly discussed her decision. The young coach told Frese she didn't want her to leave but wanted her to be happy. If Frese changed her mind and wanted to return to Tucson, Olkowski said, she would save a spot on the team for her.

Frese appreciated Olkowski's approach but had no intention of returning to Arizona. Upon reaching home, she traveled with her parents to the University of Iowa, where they met with the women's coach,

Vivian Stringer, who told Frese she was very excited about the prospect of adding an in-state player to the roster. Frese left Iowa City convinced she was going to be a Hawkeye, but a second meeting with Stringer a week and a half later changed that. Frese traveled alone to meet Stringer the second time, and the coach told her, after watching tape, she was 10 pounds overweight and too slow. She wanted Frese to join the team, but it would have to be as a walk-on with only the possibility of earning a scholarship.

Frese left the meeting blown away. She wasn't going to Iowa as a walk-on, though her parents were more than willing to pay for her to go. Frese worked harder than ever to hone her game and improve her conditioning, and she also started down the path that helped lead her into coaching that summer. Frese worked at a Blue Star camp in Terre Haute, Ind., where she met Flynn, who was impressed with her work ethic. She started working Blue Star camps across the country, introducing herself to as many coaches as possible.

As the summer neared its end, Frese realized as much as she loved her family and Iowa, things had changed in her year away. She wasn't in high school anymore, and many of her friends had moved on. Frese also missed the friends she made in Arizona. It took Frese awhile to muster up the courage to contact Olkowski — she called and hung up several times — but with her heart pounding, asked if she could return to the Wildcats. True to her word, Olkowski welcomed Frese back and said they'd just act as if everybody had amnesia.

The decision broke her parents' hearts for a second time, but Frese returned to Tucson primed for a big season and delivered. Starting every game as a sophomore, Frese averaged 13.7 points and seemed on her way to stardom, though the Wildcats struggled to a 12-17 record. The following summer she was selected to play with a Pac-10 all-star team on a two-week tour of Germany. Things couldn't have been going much better. She played well on the trip and was having dreams of playing professionally overseas after graduation.

After Frese returned from the trip, Olkowski pulled her aside and told her she needed to take at least a week off to give her body a rest. Frese, feeling better than she ever had in her life, thought her coach was crazy. She rested for two days and resumed working out. By the time October arrived, Frese began experiencing pain in her left foot. The pain, which spread to her right foot, became unbearable. After months of MRIs, cortisone shots and trips to the doctor, it was eventually determined that Frese didn't have bursa sacs in her feet. The bursa sac reduces friction between tendons and bones but through overuse and genetics, Frese lost hers. As result, her Achilles tendon was rubbing on bone, and her junior season was wrecked.

Frese eventually underwent surgery on both feet at the same time, a decision that left her with matching casts and dependent on a wheelchair for transportation. The procedure was supposed to alleviate the pain, but it didn't work. After redshirting during the 1990-91 season, she attempted to return to the court the following year, but the pain in her feet continued to worsen and her season and, ultimately, career ended after 13 games. Frese averaged 10.2 points during those 13 games, but statistics were the least of her concerns. By the time she stopped playing, she was experiencing a near-constant burning sensation in her feet and often sat in class with tears in her eyes, wondering if and when the pain would subside. In the following months, Frese went to numerous doctors without relief. Basketball, which had been the most important part of her life beyond family, was no longer a priority. Frese feared she would be forced to deal with debilitating foot pain the rest of her life.

Help came in the form of a familiar face when Flynn recommended a world-class podiatrist in Philadelphia. An examination revealed the first surgery was unsuccessful. The podiatrist performed two separate operations on her feet, preventing Frese from being immobilized by two casts at once and allowing him to evaluate the success of one procedure before moving to the next foot. Much to Frese's relief, the surgery was a success and when one foot was sufficiently healed, she had the other one repaired.

Frese had lived in pain for nearly two years, and her playing days were done. But her feet now were pain-free and have remained that way unless a big rain is coming or she gets overly stressed. The time away from basketball gave her plenty of time to think about what she wanted to do with the rest of her life. Her conclusion wasn't surprising: If she couldn't play basketball, she wanted to coach. So the women's basketball office at Pima Community College received a call from a young woman looking to get her start in the game in the fall of 1992.

––––––––––

Brenda's family hated to see her career end because of injuries, but they hadn't seen the last of her on the court. Each year when the Frese kids return home for Christmas, they head to the basketball court. When they were younger they played outside the house, but with age comes wisdom, and they eventually moved the family game to the local YMCA to escape the cold weather.

The YMCA has become so accustomed to the annual battle royale that it calls the Frese family in advance to ask when they are coming. The game has expanded exponentially and now includes husbands, wives, children and other family members. Bill and Donna rotate between officiating and keeping score, and Marsha supplies Illinois jerseys for everyone but Brenda, who refuses to wear Illini colors.

For at least one day a year, the first family of Cedar Rapids athletics reconvenes. The competition has softened over the years — during her first season at Maryland, Brenda wrenched her back in the holiday game, forcing her to dial back her effort in coming years — but winning still matters in the Frese household. That's why Brenda complains about Marsha choosing the rosters.

Chapter 11

"I'm a Team Player"

Maryland was a confident team. From the moment they arrived on campus in late August, the Terps talked of making it to the Final Four and winning a national championship. Those were the goals Frese sold players on during the recruiting process so their expectations weren't surprising. Whether Maryland could overcome its inexperience — an excuse the players refused to use — and lack of NCAA Tournament experience was uncertain, but it didn't hurt to think big. It hadn't been that long since Frese had taken over at Ball State, believing she was on her way to the top of the game. Never mind that most neutral observers would have said the job was much closer to a coach-killer than a springboard to bigger things. The Cardinals hadn't won since George H.W. Bush was in the Oval Office, but Frese believed. If her team thought it was going to go to the Final Four in 2006, she wasn't going to stop them from dreaming big. Frese had been doing it for years.

As January passed, Maryland's dream seemed to be losing traction. The Terps were winning, but their play stagnated. The team's struggles on the road at Virginia and Virginia Tech were one thing, but the miserable first half against Georgia Tech and being forced to overtime against Wake Forest sent up red flags. Parity in women's basketball had increased dramatically in the previous decade, but the talent gap between the top five to seven teams and the rest of the nation remained substantial. Elite teams often cruised through large portions of their schedule facing few challenges.

To put Maryland's "struggles" in perspective, it needed two overtimes during four straight victories while never winning by more than eight points. Though the Terps were piling up victories, they didn't appear to be closing the gap on Duke and North Carolina, the league's best teams. Playing in the ACC, the best league in women's basketball during the 2005-06 season, the Tar Heels beat conference opponents by a staggering average of 17.4 points, and Duke waxed ACC teams by 16. The Terps, by contrast, beat conference foes by 8.2 points a game, an impressive margin but not nearly the dominance displayed by North Carolina and Duke.

Frese tried everything to pull her team out of its funk. She coddled the players, threatened 6 a.m. practices, and questioned their willingness to accept the responsibility of being a top 10 team. Frese debated moves with her staff and brainstormed with her husband, who serves as an independent sounding board, before concluding Maryland needed lineup changes. But there wasn't unanimity on the staff over shaking up the lineup. The Terps started Coleman, Perry, Langhorne, Newman and Doron over a 12-1 stretch, but Frese felt the lineup needed to be tweaked.

With the exception of Langhorne and, to a lesser degree, Coleman, everyone was struggling, but Frese dialed in on Harper. The torn Achilles tendon, more than 13 months in the rearview mirror, changed her role on the team. Before the injury, Harper was nearly Langhorne's equal in the middle, grabbing rebounds, blocking shots and showing a deft shooting touch. In short, she appeared on the way to being the star Frese expected.

In the wake of Harper's injury, Langhorne's game soared, as did her role as the team's centerpiece. When Harper returned, she needed to find her place on a team that had changed dramatically in her absence. Her recovery from the injury was handled with the greatest of care, maybe too much. Frese conceded monitoring Harper's every move in preseason practice, wondering about the health of her gifted sophomore.

Harper played well in the Virgin Islands, particularly against Tennessee, when she finished with 13 points, 12 rebounds, 4 assists and 3 blocks, but struggled to maintain her level of play. By the time Maryland was in its January doldrums, Harper seemed to be regressing. She fouled out against Virginia Tech in just five minutes, failing to score for the only time in her career. In the next game against Georgia Tech, she took only two shots in 17 minutes. Harper was too talented to be playing that way, and Frese thought she knew the source of the problem. In talking to her husband at home one evening — he's a "great listener," in her words — it occurred to Frese that Harper was settling for being a good player on most nights but not a great one. If the Terps were going to achieve their goals, Harper needed to be more than good.

"It dawned on me Harp was playing second fiddle because she was coming off the bench," Frese said. "I wondered if she was settling into a comfort zone." Following the Wake Forest game, Frese had a DVD of Harper's best moments of the season assembled, and asked Harper to come to the coach's office for a meeting. Harper didn't know what to expect, saying, "The team had developed without me being there. I knew I was having a mediocre season. I was playing a little passive."

When Harper arrived in Frese's office, the coach popped in the DVD with clips of Harper playing at the peak of her abilities. She was blocking shots, running the floor, and playing with the infectious passion transferable to teammates. When the showing ended, Frese told Harper that was the type of player she recruited to College Park and wanted to see again. Instead of blaming Harper for her struggles, Frese shouldered some of the responsibility.

"I apologized to her because I had kind of mishandled her as a coach and put kid gloves on her [after the injury]," Frese said. "I told her we recruited her as an impact player, to be a star. We needed her to play at the level she was capable of."

For the emotional Harper, the meeting was a seminal one. She entered Frese's ground-floor office in Comcast with her confidence at an all-time low and left feeling recharged. "I'll never forget that the rest of my life," Harper said. "She said, 'This is you [making plays on the DVD]. Where is your confidence?' Knowing Coach B had that much confidence in me, I was like, 'I can do this.' I didn't know what the coaches thought of my game. To have the head coach take the time to do that made things much more comfortable for me."

Harper moved into the starting lineup and played her best game of the season to date with 19 points and nine rebounds in an 88-77 home win against Miami on Feb. 1. The Terps weren't great, but it was the best they had played in two weeks.

The insertion of Harper into the starting lineup wasn't the only change Frese made for the Hurricanes game. Toliver, who started the first seven games before developing shin problems, had slowly worked her way back into shape. Frese was ready to re-insert her into the lineup, allowing Doron to return to her preferred role of shooting guard.

December was a month of turmoil for Toliver, but she worked her way through the mess in January, though progress wasn't always as fast as she would have preferred. She played only a total of 39 minutes against Duke and Boston College while regaining her conditioning and establishing a new rhythm with her teammates. Toliver was frustrated with her limited contributions in the early part of the month, but Frese was encouraged that Toliver reached out to chat about the frustration — something the guard wouldn't have done a month earlier.

One night at home, Frese was online when Toliver sent her an instant message, one of her favorite forms of communication. The two had a long "chat," and Toliver opened up about her frustrations, telling her coach no one knew who she was. Frese encouraged her to work harder and counseled Toliver to be patient because in due time her name would become familiar to everybody.

After the eight-day break following the Duke game, Toliver saw her minutes begin to increase, and her shins were no longer giving her problems. With postseason play on the horizon, Frese felt the time was right to return the only true point guard to the lineup.

The difficult part was removing two others players from the starting lineup. Frese was forced to tell Perry and Newman they were returning to the bench. They were two of the team's stronger defenders and though both were struggling at the time, the move had more to do with fitting players into roles that best served the team's needs than on-court performance.

Frese's conversation with Newman was gut-wrenching. Newman did everything she was asked, and Frese was asking her to sacrifice the limelight. It wasn't any easier to tell Perry, who moved into the lineup as a freshman when Harper was injured and provided a blue-collar presence in the paint. Though the move would be viewed by fans and the media as a demotion for Perry and Newman, Frese told them that wasn't the case. She assured them their minutes wouldn't be significantly affected. Maryland had seven starters, regardless of whose name was called in pregame introductions.

For all of Maryland's talent, it didn't have much depth, making the lineup changes riskier. If Newman and Perry didn't accept their new roles, it could disrupt the entire team, but Frese knew the two well enough to be confident that wouldn't happen. Both players grew up in small towns in the South and came to Maryland to win, something that was clearly illustrated in Newman's meeting with Frese.

"It really wasn't difficult," Newman said of the move to the bench. "Once the coaches came to me and asked me about it, I said, 'I don't have a problem with that. I understand and agree. I'm a team player.' "

Perry and Newman, the target of constant barbs from teammates because of their down-home accents, embraced their new roles. "I loved coming off the bench and being a spark," Perry said. "Me and New-New [Newman's nickname] always talked about that."

Perry accepted her move to the bench, knowing there are more important things than having your name called to start a basketball game. Outside of Noirez, no Terp had made a bigger adjustment to life in College Park than Perry. Living in a small town isn't for everyone, but there often is a kinship in rural communities that suburban dwellers miss. Perry didn't grow up next to a three-story mall with a 12-theatre Cineplex, but her teammates likely didn't enjoy the hometown support Perry did in Central City, Ky.

When Frese and Walz went to Central City for Perry's home visit, which was more like a celebration given that she had already verbaled, they were told there would be a gathering in the basement hall of her church. Frese assumed it would include a small group of influential people in Perry's life. Instead, more than 100 people crowded into the basement to celebrate. Perry and her mother spoke, as did the preacher, Frese and others. It was probably the most emotional visit of Frese's career, and it provided a unique insight into Perry's world. The people in Central City were like a family, a role now filled by her teammates, and she wasn't going to be a disruptive force.

As Perry made the adjustment to College Park, she was forced to deal with difficult offcourt circumstances. She is very close to her mother Gwendolyn and older sister, Jasmine, both of whom were college athletes and faced tremendous personal challenges. In Perry's freshman year, her mother, who at one point feared she would never see her daughter play in a Maryland uniform, battled cancer. The disease went into remission, momentarily easing Perry's mind, but on May 19, 2005, tragedy struck the family again. Jasmine had enlisted in the Army after college and was training to go to Iraq when a freak accident in a Hummer broke the femur bone in both legs. Her sister had 18-inch rods inserted in each, but the nerve damage in her left leg was so catastrophic that it was amputated below the knee in the summer of 2006.

Though Perry battled adversity, she often did so with a smile on her face. Regarded as one of the team's funnier players, Perry never lacked for one-liners or T-shirts that kept her teammates laughing. Her favorite shirt said, "Drink apple juice, because O.J. will kill you."

On the court, a Perry screen occasionally felt like it would kill you. With a bench press that tops out close to 200 pounds, Perry is the team's strongest player and the one teammates least want to face in pickup games. Playing against her was rough, as Langhorne found out when an inadvertent Perry elbow left her needing nine stitches in her chin.

Frese isn't a coach who has a meeting a week, but after talking with several players individually, she called the top seven in the rotation together to discuss the state of the team before the Miami game. The players gathered in Frese's office, which is very much in tune with her personality. It's a nice office but not extravagant and certainly isn't loaded with Frese memorabilia. Her 2002 AP Coach of the Year trophy sits on a filing cabinet about as far away from her desk as the office will allow, along with a few other coaching mementos.

Frese got exactly what she wanted from the meeting. The development of leadership and accountability were two things the coaching staff hoped would grow as the season went along, and those things started to crystallize in the meeting. Players took ownership of the meeting, particularly Newman, Doron, Harper and Langhorne. They candidly discussed the team's lack of emotion and the need to begin playing better. The Terps felt they won the close games in January because Maryland was the better team but also were fortunate not to have dropped a game or two. A good season was assured, but the Terps were in search of a great season.

The meeting wasn't about individual criticism. The goal was to identify why the team hadn't played to its potential in recent weeks. The consensus was that more emotion was needed. Maryland fed off emotion but was almost entirely dependent on Langhorne and Doron to provide the spark. Harper was always full of energy, but it was time to bring a more consistent level of play to the court. Coleman and Toliver were freshmen, but that wasn't going to be an excuse. Perry and Newman knew what their new jobs would be and resolved to do them well.

There was immediate improvement. After the Miami game, the Terps beat Virginia by 14 at home in a game that showed both sides of the team. Maryland played its best basketball in more than a month in rolling to a 21-point first-half lead. However, the Terps didn't maintain their level of play and let the Cavaliers close within six points in the second half before putting them away. The win ran the team's streak to seven games and set up a showdown at North Carolina. The subsequent overtime win in Chapel Hill turned Maryland's season as the Terps overcame a month of uneven play to beat the No. 1 team in the land. It was a validating win for the players. They weren't just talking about being good, they were good.

Four days after beating the No. 1 Tar Heels, Maryland returned to Tobacco Road to play Duke, the new No. 1. team in the nation. The Terps had offcourt business to tend to first, though. The night before the game, Maryland dined at Maggiano's, an Italian restaurant in Durham, N.C., with dessert provided for the first time all season. The game was televised on ESPN2, and Frese challenged her squad to become the first team in the history of college basketball — male or female — to beat top-ranked teams in consecutive games. The Terps immediately showed they were much improved since the earlier 18-point shellacking by Duke at College Park. Maryland attacked Duke in a way that it hadn't during Frese's tenure, taking a 41-33 lead into the half, but the Blue Devils roared back to win when an old problem resurfaced.

"Do you know how many points they scored in the second half? Fifty-seven points," Frese told her team afterward. "I'm not faulting your effort. I thought you played hard. But there is a fine line of separation why they are No. 1 in the country and we are No. 4. Well, I want to be No. 1, and I know you want to be No. 1."

The loss to the hated Blue Devils, the Terps' 14th straight in the series, was disappointing but not discouraging. In January, the gulf between Maryland and Duke had seemed as wide as the distance between College Park and Durham. By Feb. 13, Frese was talking to her team about a fine line of separation.

The loss to the Blue Devils didn't kill Maryland's momentum, as Boston College learned three days later. In their most impressive performance of the season, the Terps pulverized the 18th-ranked Eagles 86-59. Maryland led by more than 30 points for much of the second half, and the narrow victories of January were a thing of the past.

One night after defeating Miami, the Terps showed up at the Comcast Center wearing their jerseys, but it wasn't their night to play under the lights. As a capacity crowd streamed into the building for the game between the Maryland and North Carolina men, Frese's Terps were working the concourse at Comcast to collect money to fight breast cancer. The Terps would be playing at N.C. State in a game dubbed Hoops for Hope on Feb. 19. The Wolfpack were coached by Kay Yow, a legendary figure in the game and the sister of Maryland Athletics Director Debbie Yow. Kay Yow was diagnosed with cancer in 1987 but subsequently was free of the disease until it returned in 2005. Debbie Yow wasn't the impetus for Maryland's decision to raise the money. It was the choice of Frese and her team, which had been touched directly by the disease through the battle of Perry's mother.

The Terps presented a check for more than $4,000 in a ceremony before the game in Raleigh, but their goodwill ended there. N.C. State played an inspired game before Maryland, led by the blossoming Harper's 20 points, earned a 65-57 win that pleased their coach.

Maryland closed regular season play in the ACC with an 89-63 pasting of Clemson as Coleman made her first five three-pointers en route to a game-high 20 points and Langhorne became the fastest player in Maryland history to reach the 1,000-point plateau. The Terps finished ACC play 12-2 and tied for second place, their best finish since 1993.

One of the season's prevailing themes was Maryland's youth, but the regular-season finale against Northern Colorado was about age and experience. Carr and Ross, the team's only seniors, didn't play a lot of minutes throughout the season but brought a unique perspective to the team. The Terps' players heard a lot about Frese's 10-18 first season, but only Carr and Ross experienced it. The duo both started as freshmen, but as Maryland's talent level increased their playing time decreased.

Carr, a tri-captain, enjoyed more court time her senior year and always played with intensity, while Ross' chances for earning significant time ended with her broken kneecap before the season. Senior Night against Northern Colorado was their chance to enjoy the spotlight. For Ross, the game marked her first start since freshman year. The two enjoyed their first extended playing time since December as the Terps waltzed to an 89-53 win against the overmatched Bears.

Maryland's preseason Final Four talk seemed more plausible with each passing day, and there was no better preparation for the Big Dance than the ACC Tournament, which included three of the nation's top four ranked teams. Now Frese and her staff began to see a difference in practice. The scout team, comprised of male students, suddenly was being defeated with much greater ease, and communication was greatly improved. The Terps were ready for postseason play.

Chapter 12

'EKUD'

A s the NCAA Tournament field expanded over the years, the importance of conference tournaments waned, at least at the game's highest level. The winner of the ACC Tournament was crowned conference champion and received an automatic NCAA bid, but there wasn't a tremendous sense of urgency for a team like Maryland. The Terps finished the regular season at 26-3, and were a lock for an invitation.

When Maryland boarded a charter flight to Greensboro, N.C., for the ACC Tournament, the Terps very much wanted to win the event and earn a No. 1 NCAA Tournament seed, but it wasn't going to make their season. Before the ACC Tournament, now four days because of expansion, the league announced its postseason honors and the Terps were well represented like most years under Frese. Coleman put together a sensational season, ranking among the top 10 in six statistical categories, and was named ACC Rookie of the Year. She was second on the team in rebounding, averaging 8.1, and led the ACC in three-point field goal percentage at 47 percent. Coleman had the strength to be a dominant rebounder and the skill to play the perimeter, making her a match-up nightmare. The second straight Terp to win rookie of the year honors, following Langhorne, Coleman was named to the all-rookie team and was a second-team all-ACC selection, the only freshman in the league to be named all-ACC.

Langhorne was a first-team all-conference selection, and Doron garnered second-team honors. Toliver, who had elevated her game dramatically in February, averaging 13.8 points, earned all-rookie honors as well.

The Terps, who received an opening-round bye, played Georgia Tech in the quarterfinals, and for at least one player, the opportunity to play in the ACC Tournament wasn't something to be taken for granted.

On the ride to Greensboro Coliseum for a late-night practice, Harper, who had been denied the opportunity to play in the 2005 tournament because of the Achilles injury, was overcome by emotion. At the end of practice after midnight on game day, Harper addressed her teammates, telling them they had to play as if every game in the tournament could be their last.

Maryland was playing its best basketball of the season down the stretch, but the stakes were rising and the team's intensity needed to keep pace. In an attempt to drive home the importance of elevating the level of play, Frese brought in a special friend of the program to deliver a pregame talk to her players. The Oakland Raiders' LaMont Jordan, a follower of the women's program since his days as a star running back in College Park, continued to support the team long after he headed for the National Football League. He had donated $25,000 the past two years and took pride in the team's success. The Maryland players, in turn, admired him and respected his words, which made his speech all the more poignant.

In a talk that sounded as if it could have occurred in a NFL locker room, Jordan praised the players for their success but challenged them by name to do more. Jordan told Toliver she provided another gear but it also was her responsibility to settle the offense when it was out of sync. He challenged Harper to bring energy to the paint, told Doron to battle through a thigh injury and implored Newman, who was struggling with her shot, "There is no shooting slump."

The players hung on Jordan's every word and his concluding ones gave them chills: "You have the ability, ladies. Y'all can go out there and run with anybody. You have to make it up in your mind that's what you want to do. I believe in you guys. I'm having a good time. I'm slapping hands with people I don't even know, and they are slapping hands with people they don't know. You know why they are doing it? For you."

Jordan's talk sent the Terps from a meeting room at the Sheraton Hotel on a high, but Georgia Tech once again made life difficult. With Harper struggling to rein in her emotions and finishing with just three points and six rebounds, the Yellow Jackets battled Maryland to the wire. Coleman scored the Terps' last six points in a 71-66 victory that was in doubt until the closing seconds. It wasn't a pretty win, but Maryland executed with precision when it was most needed and advanced to play in the semifinals.

Next up — Duke.

Frese isn't normally superstitious, but as part of her pregame preparations, team manager Kim Lynch styled and dried and straightened her hair. Lynch, a senior, had been with Frese from the beginning, and she took responsibility for Frese's hair as a freshman. The talk between the two was generally light, with Frese always accepting hair care tips. As Lynch prepared Frese's hair following the loss at Duke in February, the talk turned to basketball, and she said something that stuck with Frese: Maryland's biggest problem against the Blue Devils was the name on the front of the jersey.

When Maryland played Duke, it was always different, and everyone associated with the program felt it. The attendance wasn't where Frese or her players wanted it to be most of the season, but when the Blue Devils came to town, the spotlight shined most brightly on them. Students who didn't otherwise pay much attention suddenly cared, and the Maryland players knew what a win would mean to the program.

The Terps used the Duke game as a measuring stick — a rabbit to chase, so to speak — and as a result approached the Blue Devils differently than other teams on the schedule. Maryland hadn't conceded anything to North Carolina and Tennessee, but it hadn't been as resilient in the face of a challenge from Duke. Bernabei was the coach responsible for scouting the Blue Devils, and Frese challenged her to take a different approach if the two teams met again. Bernabei, displaying the creativity that serves her so well on the recruiting trail, delivered a scouting report unlike any the Terps had seen.

Maryland scouting reports have the opponent, time, and date listed at the top, followed by information on the opposing team's personnel. As the Terps prepared for their third game of the season against the Blue Devils, they knew who they were facing. Lindsey Harding, Wanisha Smith, Monique Currie and friends were familiar names to the Maryland players, which made the scouting report all the funnier.

The report Bernabei handed the players was amusingly headed:

"Ekud, 3:30 Saturday, March 4th, 2006." It went on to profile a talented Ekud lineup that featured the likes of "Lori Higgins," "Wanda Schmit" and "Monica Carry." It didn't take the Maryland players long to figure out what Bernabei had done. "Ekud" is Duke spelled backwards, of course, and the players' names closely approximated the Blue Devils' lineup. The Terps players got a laugh out of the ploy while the point of the report was driven home: Duke was just another team, and Maryland had to approach the game as such.

"Playing against Duke was psychological," Langhorne said. "I think it was in our heads because we were like, 'It's Duke, it's Duke.'

[Bernabei] was like, 'I want you guys to realize they are just another team.' "

Maryland, ranked fourth in the nation entering the tournament, dominated the game's first 27 minutes. The Blue Devils never led in the first half as Maryland, which shot 55 percent from the field, took a 38-32 lead into the break. The Terps continued to attack in the opening minutes of the second half, gaining a 53-38 lead on a jumper by Perry with 13:32 remaining. Duke then put together one of its patented runs, outscoring the Terps 16-0 over the next 3:38 to take its first lead at 54-53.

During Duke's 14-game winning streak against the Terps, Maryland often failed to answer the Blue Devils' runs. The Terps didn't quit in those games, but they never responded with the confidence and aggression necessary to overtake a team like Duke. With the Blue Devils erasing a game's worth of Terrapins domination in a run that occurred with frightening speed, another Duke win could have been a formality.

But Maryland was a far different squad than the one Duke blew out in January and handled down the stretch in February. With a pro-Duke crowd of 10,019 in a frenzy, the Terps responded with a blitz of their own. Langhorne took a pass from Toliver and converted a quick layup, making the score 55-54 and erasing Duke's lead. Then Harper took over. Less than 24 hours removed from one of her worst games of the year, she scored seven straight points, including a three-point play that left her and her teammates roaring. Langhorne book-ended the run with another layup to push the Maryland lead to 62-54. Duke never came closer than six points the rest of the way.

Maryland 78, Duke 70.

Fourteen games and more than six years of frustration had ended. Harper led the Terps with 17 points while Coleman continued her stellar play with 16 points, 13 rebounds and 4 assists. The Terps were ecstatic. The one mental hurdle they hadn't cleared was Duke, and that obstacle was now vanquished.

When Maryland returned to the Sheraton, supporters filled the lobby, loudly cheering as the team made its way through an opening in the crowd. The Terps exchanged high fives with their fans, but one member of the team was missing. Team manager Andre Lane wasn't feeling well and fell asleep on the bus on the way back to the hotel. In a joyous ride home, nobody noticed that Lane hadn't gotten off the bus. The team made its way through the crowded lobby and headed upstairs to eat pizza while Lane got locked on the bus. He was finally able to get in touch with Floyd, who found the driver and got Lane off the bus, but not before providing the team with a good laugh.

———————————————

The victory put the Terps in their first ACC Tournament final since 1994 and waiting for them was a North Carolina team hungry for revenge. The Tar Heels, who had defeated Duke twice, once more were atop the national polls at 29-1, their lone loss to Maryland.

The game was played at a frantic pace, something both teams preferred. Maryland played well in spurts, but it was North Carolina's day. Langhorne and Harper dominated the interior against Duke, but the Tar Heels turned the tables on them. Erlana Larkins scored 26 points and grabbed 12 rebounds to power UNC to a 91-80 win. Maryland was within 79-76 with 5:22 left, but the Tar Heels were the better team this time. The difference in the game was North Carolina's 48-37 advantage on the boards and 58 points in the paint. Maryland, with Doron still hobbled by injury, didn't play its best game. Langhorne's struggles (12 points on 3 of 7 shooting) were uncharacteristic, and Toliver missed 8 of 9 shots and scored four points, but some of the credit for the poor play went to North Carolina. Maryland was disappointed with the loss, but as Toliver told Harper afterward, the Terps couldn't get greedy and expect two titles.

With NCAA Selection Monday nine days away, Maryland headed home to College Park brimming with confidence. The experience the Terps had gained playing Duke and North Carolina in consecutive games for the second time was invaluable.

The Terps, who climbed to No. 3 in both national polls, their highest ranking since 1993, after the ACC Tournament were going to carry a record of 28-4 into the NCAA Tournament. Maryland hadn't lost to a team ranked lower than No. 2 at the time of the meeting. With a sterling record in the country's best league and wins against North Carolina and Duke to their credit, the Terps were hopeful about their chances of receiving a No. 1 seed in the 2006 NCAA Tournament.

Chapter 13

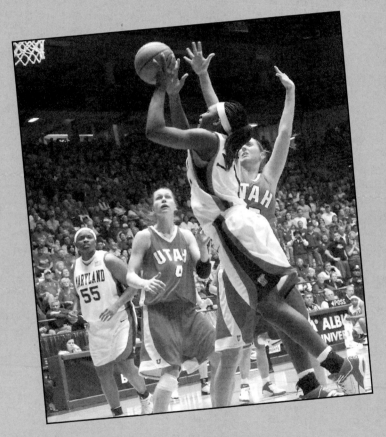

The Journey Begins

B etween the ACC and NCAA Tournaments, the Terps didn't play a game for 15 days — by far their longest break of the season. Coming off three games in three days at the ACC Tournament, Frese gave the players several days off, requiring no more than light conditioning work. Still, excitement was building.

Two years earlier, the Terps, who were on the bubble, had hosted a selection show viewing party. Frese could still vividly recall her panic attack moments before the show started, fretting over what she would tell the crowd if Maryland wasn't invited to the Big Dance. In 2005, the Terps were a No. 7 seed, solidly in the tournament but an afterthought on the national scene. Now ESPN dispatched a crew to College Park to interview players and coaches for its selection show special and tournament coverage. The network, which televised every game of the tournament, devoted special attention to the top teams in the field, and that group now included Maryland.

ESPN's attention might have been routine in other places, but the Terps, still new to the national spotlight, enjoyed their star turn. They laughed, told stories, danced for the cameras and reveled in the exposure. They were going to enjoy the NCAAs and everything that went with it.

While the players rested, Maryland's coaches continued to grind. A couple days off from practice meant Frese could hit the recruiting trail, though it was increasingly difficult for her to attend a game without attracting attention. With her trademark blond hair and red Maryland attire, Frese was an easily identifiable presence. Success had done a lot of things to and for the Terps, but reducing their zeal on the recruiting trail wasn't one of them.

Frese also found time to sneak out one evening with Floyd to go in search of new clothing. Floyd, by the unanimous acclaim of the Maryland players, was the best dressed coach on staff and the friend Frese turned to for fashion help. Frese wasn't in search of the latest spring fashion, merely two outfits that would be worn only if the Terps were playing in the Final Four in Boston. The two haggled over the colors she should choose, with Frese favoring outfits in Terps hues. Floyd prevailed, convincing Frese her goal was to be the best-dressed coach in Boston, not the one who best matched her team's uniforms. In a six-month season filled with long days and short nights, the shopping excursion was a relaxing respite. Frese had dreamed of coaching in the Final Four since she started in the profession, and buying a couple of outfits for Boston was as enjoyable a way to continue pushing herself toward that goal as any.

The tournament field was announced on Monday, March 13, and Maryland invited the program's closest supporters to a viewing party in Heritage Hall in the Comcast Center. The Terps felt their profile warranted strong consideration for a No. 1 seed. North Carolina, Duke and SEC regular-season champion LSU were considered locks for three of the four top seeds. Tennessee, 28-4 entering the tournament, was the team many observers thought might nudge the Terps out for the final one. Frese addressed the crowd before the show, saying Maryland's seed wasn't nearly as important as the way the team was playing. She was correct in her assessment. NCAA Tournament seeding, while great for water cooler debate, wasn't nearly as important as the type of draw a team received, but it was important to the Terps and their supporters.

While the team was one victory shy of the most in a season in program history, the Terps felt underappreciated outside of their core group of supporters. Duke and North Carolina received all the plaudits, and most of what was said about the Terps followed this familiar line: They are talented, but too young to win.

As ESPN announced the brackets, a wave of excitement swept the viewing party when Tennessee was awarded the No. 2 seed in the Cleveland Region, opposite North Carolina. An air of expectation enveloped Heritage Hall as each region was unveiled. The Cleveland, Bridgeport and San Antonio brackets were announced, and Maryland's name had yet to be called as the anticipation grew. A collective groan went up when Ohio State, the Big Ten regular-season and tournament champion, was announced as the No. 1 seed in the Albuquerque Region. The Buckeyes entered the tournament with a 27-2 record, but their strength of schedule and quality wins didn't compare with Maryland's. Moments later, the Terps' quadrant of the bracket was announced. Maryland received a No. 2 seed and would open against No. 15 Sacred Heart in State College, Pa.

The team was disappointed, feeling it had been deprived of the prestige that accompanies a top seed, but as far as Frese was concerned, things couldn't have been much better. From a motivational point of view, she got to play the no-respect card with her players, but most importantly the Terps received a very good draw. If both teams advanced through the draw, Ohio State wasn't nearly as daunting as the other three No. 1 seeds — Duke, UNC and LSU — and Maryland played the first two rounds in nearby Pennsylvania, making travel for the team and its fans relatively easy.

Maryland's game with Sacred Heart was on March 19, and the Terps resumed normal practices the day of the selection show. The primary emphasis was defense and rebounding, the same components Frese had stressed since the beginning of preseason. As another one of her motivational ploys, Frese gave the team "40 Minutes of Shell" T-shirts with "Boston '06" on the sleeve. The saying was a takeoff on the "40 Minutes of Hell" motto the Arkansas men had used under Nolan Richardson in the 1990s, and the players loved it. In this case, "40 Minutes of Shell" was code for defend and rebound and your chances of going to Boston are very good.

Frese was candid with her players, telling them their draw was a good one. Ohio State had knocked the Terps out of the 2005 tournament, and a chance to exact revenge on the Buckeyes was appealing. Unlike the previous two years, when Maryland had to be at its best to advance out of the first round, the Terps had some breathing room against Sacred Heart. The Pioneers, 26-4 and Northeast Conference champs, were making their first appearance in the NCAA Tournament. They were a scrappy, well-coached team, but all the pluck and sideline genius in the world couldn't overcome Maryland's superior talent.

Maryland's biggest concern heading into the game might have been the prospect of playing at Penn State, a place that had been a house of horrors for Maryland athletics. The Terps' football team was 1-35-1 all-time against the Nittany Lions, and the women's basketball team had absorbed a 101-74 loss there in Frese's first season. The Terps took a winding three-hour bus ride to get to State College, and the area's bad karma didn't take long to resurface.

With little to do beyond practice, Coleman and Newman were engaged in tickling horseplay with team manager Lynch. As she tried to break away from her tormentors, Lynch heard her elbow pop. Accompanied by a sheepish Coleman and Newman, she went to trainer Mark Charvat's room, and when she took her sweatshirt off, it revealed an obviously dislocated elbow. Charvat and Lynch were off to the emergency room until 2 a.m., Coleman and Newman felt horrible, and Frese was without her pregame hairdresser. Fortunately, Lynch had someone ready to step in. Under Lynch's watchful eye, Brittney Renehan, another team manager and a freshman, was able to handle the responsibility of styling and straightening Frese's hair. With order restored, Maryland was ready to open play in the 2006 NCAA Tournament.

"This is what we've worked so hard for: the big dance," Frese told her team in the locker room. "This is what it's all about; this is the big stage. I'm telling you, you go out there and dictate 40 minutes of hell ... I mean shell."

The crowd at Bryce Jordan Center was only 3,990, but the atmosphere was different than a regular-season game. When the Terps took the court to warm up, they were serenaded by chants of "overrated" by a small but boisterous group of Sacred Heart fans. The Pioneers and their fans were in their first NCAA Tournament and pushing a needle.

Sacred Heart started just one player over 5-10, but was as scrappy as advertised. The Terps controlled the action throughout the game, but the Pioneers, after hitting a three-pointer at the buzzer, went into the half trailing 47-33, which still put them within range of heavily favored Maryland. After playing in spurts in the opening 20 minutes, Maryland put on a second-half clinic, opening with a 21-2 run that pushed its lead to 68-35. All 10 Maryland players got on the court, and nine played at least 13 minutes. Led by Langhorne, Perry and Harper, Maryland scored 56 points in the paint in a 95-54 romp. The Terps played closer to 25 minutes of shell than 40, but their objectives were met.

The tournament began in earnest for Maryland in the second round, the point at which it had stumbled the previous two years. Though the losses to LSU in 2004 and Ohio State in 2005 were expected, at least by outside observers, the challenge of clearing the second-round hurdle hung over Maryland's head. Awaiting the Terps in round two was St. John's of the Big East Conference. The Red Storm bore some similarities to the Terps. They had a young coach, Kim Barnes Arico, who had revived a previously moribund program and had very good athletes on the perimeter. St. John's defeated California 78-68 in the first round, and entered the Maryland game with everything to gain.

In the opening minutes, it appeared as if Maryland would blow St. John's out. Harper won the opening tip, knocking it to Toliver, who immediately fired the ball to Coleman in the left corner for a three-pointer. Harper and Langhorne scored a short time later and the Terps were up 7-0 less than two minutes in, but they were missing a spark. "If somebody had walked in and didn't look at the scoreboard, they would have never known who was up," Walz said. "We looked dead. We were just going through the motions and not really excited."

The Red Storm charged back, riding the hot shooting of guards Kia Wright, Tara Walker and Grebe Barlow. The perimeter players made 4 of 7 three-pointers in the opening half and were routinely beating Maryland off the dribble. St. John's led for considerable stretches, but the Terps took a tenuous 35-34 lead into the half. But Maryland, knowing its season would be judged a complete failure if it failed to advance out of the second round, had played a tight first half. Frese sensed they were playing scared. "This is the first time all season I've had to use the time in the locker room to settle us down, build confidence and composure," Frese said after the game. "We didn't spend a lot of time on Xs and Os. It was [a case of] trying to get them to settle down and play like a team, believe in themselves and believe in each other."

St. John's tested Maryland's belief by making its first five shots of the second half and taking a 44-38 lead, its largest of the game. With the Terps struggling to control their nerves, they turned to Langhorne. Earlier in the season, she had carried Maryland through several of its taut January games, and now Langhorne did the same against the Red Storm. Every time the Terps needed a basket, they found Langhorne, who scored 18 of her 30 points in the second half. Despite her efforts, an upset seemed a very real possibility when Wright drained a three-pointer to give St. John's a 71-69 lead with 4:51 remaining to bring an increasingly pro-St. John's crowd to its feet.

The Red Storm had a chance to extend their lead on their next possession, but Wright missed a jumper and Toliver grabbed the rebound and headed down the center of the floor. Toliver attacked the basket and fired the ball to Newman on the left wing in front of the Maryland bench. Mired in a 10-for-41 shooting slump from three-point range entering the tournament, Newman never hesitated. She caught the ball and shot, making a three-pointer that gave the Terps a 72-71 lead. The Red Storm tied the game on a free throw by Barlow, but Langhorne reasserted her dominance by scoring the game's next four points, including an offensive rebound and put-back with under a minute left that gave Maryland a 76-72 lead. St. John's battled valiantly, but it just didn't have an answer for Maryland inside. The Terps outrebounded the Red Storm 46-31, and its 18 second-chance points were the difference in an 81-74 win.

The game wasn't an artistic success, particularly for Toliver, who finished with nine points on 4-for-15 shooting, 8 assists and 6 turnovers, and Doron, who failed to make a field goal for only the third time in her college career, but Maryland was on its way to the Sweet 16 for the first time since 1992.

Maryland boarded the bus and headed back to College Park after the victory, relieved in equal parts to have survived the game and excited to be spending spring break in Albuquerque. Bus travel, while still not exciting, had enjoyed many technological advances in recent years, not the least of which was a satellite that allowed the team to watch television on the way home. Since Maryland had played an early game, the second set of NCAA Tournament games being played across the country were being televised when the Terps boarded the bus. They got to watch the end of the tournament's first major upset. Eighth-seeded Boston College, an ACC ally in this case, upset No. 1-seeded Ohio State 79-69, widening a bracket the Terps already thought was favorable.

Maryland was the highest remaining seed in the Albuquerque Region, but when ESPN returned to its studio show, there was precious little talk about the Terps, and what they did hear wasn't flattering. Maryland's defense, which wasn't good against St. John's, was criticized, and analyst Stacy Dales-Schuman quickly proclaimed the Terps' next opponent, defending national champion Baylor, her favorite to advance to the Final Four. As the players howled on the back of the bus, Walz told them the truth about their defense hurt, and Frese smiled. What more could a coach, whose team had been feeding off a perceived lack of respect, ask for?

Next up was Baylor, and the Terps had little turnaround time. They arrived in College Park in the wee hours of Wednesday morning and would be departing for Albuquerque on Thursday morning. But nobody was complaining.

The Terps' charter flight to Albuquerque, which also included cheerleaders, the pep band and boosters, was delayed for more than four hours, but it proved to be a minor inconvenience. When the plane touched down, Maryland made immediate plans to deal with the altitude in Albuquerque, a city more than 5,000 feet above sea level. The effects of the altitude weren't extreme in Albuquerque, but there was a noticeable difference. Charvat stocked each player's room with water and Gatorade and encouraged the Terps to drink four or five bottles a day to stay hydrated. The players took his advice more seriously after their first practice at The Pit, the famed arena hosting the region.

The Baylor game was the type of challenge Walz loved. Neither team had seen the other play, and both were going into their preparations with little or no knowledge of the opponent. Walz relished the opportunity to study film and devise a game plan to help the team win. Baylor and its star post player, Sophia Young, gave the Terps plenty of unsettling tape to watch. A 6-1 post player, Young was one of the game's best performers. She was a two-time Kodak All-American, the Big 12 Player of the Year and she was named the Most Outstanding Player of the 2005 Final Four after leading the Bears to their first NCAA title. Young was the Big 12 all-time leading scorer and was named to the league's all-decade team before the start of her senior season.

Baylor, the No. 3 seed in the region, suffered significant losses to graduation after winning the NCAA title, but it was a talented and improving opponent. The Bears were 26-7 and had won eight of their previous nine games before facing the Terps. Maryland knew Young, who averaged 22 points and 10 rebounds, was going to get her points but wanted to make her take between 20-25 shots to do so. The Terps wanted to force her away from the basket and defended her with Harper,

Langhorne and Perry, giving her a variety of different looks.

While much of the pregame emphasis was on Young, the game also was an opportunity for Langhorne to show the nation what her teammates and coaches believed — that she was the best post player in the country. The strength of Maryland's team was its multitude of weapons and unselfish play. The top seven players were capable of leading the team in scoring on a given night, but all sacrificed individually for the benefit of the team. At the heart of the unselfish play was Langhorne, as quiet and humble a star a coach could hope to find.

Langhorne has as many post moves as anyone in the country and a first step that often left opponents grasping at her shadow. Part of what made the Terps a great team was her ability to score on a scarcity of shots. She had led the team in scoring (17.2) and the nation in field goal percentage, making a staggering 67 percent of her shots. But statistics aren't what made Langhorne's sophomore season great. She was a rock, carrying the team when needed, and her teammates all respected her talent and work ethic.

Langhorne comes by her talent and humility honestly. She grew up in a blue-collar household, the daughter of an immigrant transit worker and a stay-at-home mom, and basketball wasn't overemphasized. The two main priorities in the Langhorne house were church and school, in that order.

Langhorne didn't play organized basketball until the eighth grade and didn't begin playing AAU ball until after the ninth grade. Once she took up the game, her parents didn't initially allow her to play on Sundays. Her two older brothers Cryhten (Maryland-Eastern Shore) and Chris (Texas State) both played low-level Division I basketball, so it wasn't unexpected when she showed an aptitude for the game. She received her first recruiting letter from Virginia Commonwealth following her debut on the AAU circuit, and others soon followed. When the nation's most prominent programs began pursuing Langhorne, Cryhten convinced their father to let young Crystal play on Sundays, something he agreed to reluctantly. "I see a lot of players whose parents were like, 'You should do this, you should do that,'" Langhorne said. "I feel like when I come home and talk to my parents, it shouldn't be about basketball, unless it's a good game."

Langhorne has never lacked for work ethic, and she quickly became a fixture on the court. Her brother worked at a local recreation center, so Langhorne practiced and played whenever she wanted. A young eighth-grader who had missed a lot of layups quickly developed into one of the nation's best players.

Frese's favorite story about Langhorne's work ethic came during her freshman season. The coaches were trying to get Langhorne, a lefty, to use her right hand more, and Frese suggested she start doing little things, like brushing her teeth and eating with her right hand, to improve her dexterity. About a week later, Langhorne told Frese she was surprised how difficult it was to brush her teeth with her right hand. Coaches make suggestions to players all the time and they are not always heeded, but Langhorne listened.

Following her freshman season, Frese told her she needed to improve at the free throw line, where she had shot just 56.7 percent. Langhorne worked all summer and improved to 67 percent as a sophomore. Another aspect of her game that emerged as a sophomore was her ability to lead. Langhorne didn't do so by chastising her teammates, but she had, with Frese's prodding, developed into one of the team's most emotional players. Unlike the girl who rarely said a word when she arrived from Willingboro, N.J., Langhorne wasn't afraid to celebrate when she or a teammate scored a big basket.

The only part of Langhorne that didn't develop was her ego. She credits her teammates with her success. She is a coach's dream, a model teammate and often the person leading the back of the bus in song and dance. Langhorne had received her share of recognition but never as much as her teammates thought she deserved. With Baylor and Young up next, she would have the opportunity to showcase her game.

———————

Baylor was coached by Kim Mulkey, who like Frese is part of a younger generation of coaches stepping to the forefront. As a player, she had helped lead Louisiana Tech to a four-year record of 130-6, won two national titles and played in two other Final Fours. Mulkey took over Baylor in 2000 and turned the Bears into a power, culminating with the 2005 NCAA title. One of the cornerstones of Baylor's success was its tenacious man-to-man defense. Mulkey didn't like to double-team people, and Langhorne would be no exception.

Maryland won the opening tip and went into its halfcourt set. As expected, Baylor matched Young up with Langhorne with no help. Toliver immediately dumped the ball into Langhorne, who spun to the middle and laid the ball in 10 seconds into the game. On Maryland's next possession, Doron found her for an open layup, and on the Terps' next two possessions Langhorne rebounded errant three-point attempts and converted them into baskets. Just 2:16 into the game, the score was Langhorne 8, Baylor 0.

After her fourth basket, Mulkey signaled for a timeout as Langhorne, making what her teammates affectionately call "The Face" yelled with delight. "The Face" is the look Langhorne has when she is screaming with joy, mouth agape, and arms often flailing. Her teammates enjoyed a few smiles while looking at "The Face" when it was displayed on the front of the Washington Post after the win against St. John's, and when Langhorne is playing with that much confidence and emotion, her team-mates feed off it.

After trailing 14-2 early, Baylor showed the tenacity of a champion by rallying to tie the game at 27 with 3:55 remaining in the half. The Bears were feeling much better about their chances, having withstood Maryland's opening barrage, but just when they appeared to be getting settled into the game, Langhorne started a surge that blew them out of it. She made two free throws to break the tie and added a layup to make the score 31-28. Doron made a pair of free throws with 41 seconds remaining, and Baylor turned the ball over at three quarters court with six-tenths of a second remaining. The Terps then planned to inbound the ball to Newman for a desperation heave. As the players were walking into position, both teams essentially waiting for the half to expire, Walz saw Langhorne walk towards the Maryland basket with just one Baylor play-er accompanying her. He immediately started screaming for her to post up. Langhorne, with the defender on her back raised her hand under-neath the basket, while Walz was yelling at Doron, the inbounder, "Throw it to Lang!" Doron lofted a perfect pass to Langhorne who caught the ball and laid it in going to her left in one motion as the buzzer sounded. The basket sent Maryland into the half with a 35-28 lead and riding a tidal wave of emotion.

Langhorne, who finished the first half with 20 points and nine rebounds, walked into the locker room complimenting Doron on the pass. With teammates buzzing about her play and discussing how many points she already had scored, Langhorne, with a smile on her face, said, "Thanks for passing me the ball, guys."

Her teammates erupted in laughter.

Maryland opened the second half with a 14-2 run to push its lead to 49-30, and the game was over. Langhorne, in arguably the tournament's most impressive individual performance, made 14 of 18 shots, scored 34 points and grabbed 15 rebounds, pulverizing Young and Baylor in the Terps' 82-63 win. On the defensive end, Maryland executed its game plan to perfection. Young scored 26 points but needed 25 shots, and most of her scoring came after the issue had been decided. With Harper's length, Perry's strength and Langhorne's all-around skill, it was difficult for the Baylor star to score.

The Terps liked to think of themselves as a team full of stars, but nobody shined brighter for them through three rounds of the NCAA Tournament than Langhorne. Now, with her leading the way, Maryland was one win from the Final Four.

Chapter 14

Dead Women Walking

A fter Maryland put the finishing touches on an 82-63 dismantling of Baylor, the defending national champion, everything seemed to be falling into place for the upstart Terps. Maryland advanced to the Elite Eight for the first time since 1992, putting one of the nation's younger teams one win from the game's biggest stage — the Final Four.

The Terps exchanged high-fives and whooped it up in the locker room, knowing they were on the cusp of fulfilling a dream and playing their best basketball of the season. They had no way of knowing the next 48 hours, which should have been among their most enjoyable as athletes, would be the most difficult of the season.

The Terps checked into the Albuquerque Marriott as healthy as they had been all year. After two days of Albuquerque's 70-degree weather, nearly cloudless skies and the dominating win against Baylor, Maryland's trip took a sickening turn, literally. Between 5:30 a.m. and 6 a.m. on Sunday morning after the Baylor game, Charvat's hotel phone rang. No good call comes that early in the morning, particularly when traveling with a bunch of college students, and this one was no different.

The trainer was rousted from bed with the news that Harper, Perry and Carr were sick. Because three players fell ill at the same time, Charvat's initial inclination was to chalk it up to food poisoning, something likely to pass and certainly not a threat to the entire team. Then strength and conditioning coach Corliss Fingers started feeling sick and Charvat recalled that a team cheerleader had fallen ill before the Baylor game. With five people sick, the Terps started asking questions of the hotel staff and learned the latter had been battling a nasty and highly contagious virus for the last week.

In an effort to stop the spread of what team doctor Yvette Rooks diagnosed as gastrointestinitis, the players, who typically stay two to a room, were given individual rooms and healthy teammates and staff avoided contact with sick players. The Utah game was still 36 hours away, and there was no panic in the Terps camp — yet.

Frese and her team, sans the ailing players, headed to The Pit for a Sunday afternoon practice and a session with the media. The Terps, who only had a 10-person roster when everybody was healthy, rearranged practice plans, but the session was closed to the media and public so nobody knew that 30 percent of the team didn't participate.

Frese and all five starters were expected to attend the post-practice press conference, but Harper's absence went unquestioned by a less than suspicious press corps. That was fine with Frese, who preferred not to disclose the sickness for competitive purposes. By Sunday evening, Harper, Perry and Carr seemed to have come through the most acute part of the illness, meaning the vomiting and diarrhea had stopped, and it became a matter of replenishing fluids and energy.

The players were no longer getting physically ill, but they weren't ready for a basketball game either. Rooks and Charvat forced them to drink fluids and eat as much as possible. The last thing that returns after such a virus is the appetite. An empty stomach to the average person isn't a big deal, but to an athlete on the eve of competition, food and the energy it provides are essential. Subway sandwiches were the only thing that sounded appealing to the trio, so they had all of it they could eat over the next 24 hours.

While the sick players were attempting to recover, the virus started sweeping through the rest of the traveling party, bringing cheerleaders, band members and boosters to their knees and raising additional concerns about a possible spread through the rest of the team. The one person not concerned about getting sick was Toliver. "I was talking to my mom in the [hotel] lobby and she said, 'There is a bug going around,'" Toliver said. "I was like, 'I'm not going to get sick. I rarely if ever get sick.'"

Ah, youthful indiscretion. The freshman tempted fate, and fate won. The team went to dinner Sunday evening, and Toliver started getting light-headed and experiencing hot flashes, her discomfort obvious enough that Charvat walked over to ask how she was feeling. The answer was not good. Toliver's mother, who made the trip to Albuquerque, came to pick her up. When Toliver got back to the hotel, she sprinted to her room before getting sick and suffered from the virus the rest of the night.

Charvat called Frese, who was having dinner with a former college teammate and friends, to tell her about Toliver, and the reaction was almost one of disbelief. Why now? Why before this game?

As Frese talked to her team trainer and bantered with friends, her own appetite was oddly missing. She hadn't eaten since breakfast and had no desire for dinner. In the early hours of Monday morning — game day — Frese was also stricken. She was sick all night, her thoughts, between trips to the bathroom, centering on the fact that she had to be ready to lead her team at 5 p.m. Walz got sick overnight as well, and the Terps had real concerns about who would be well enough to play or coach come tip-off. The customary pregame shoot-around was cancelled and film sessions were handled on a one-on-one basis with Bernabei, who had recently found out she was pregnant but hadn't disclosed the news, going to each player's room to review the scouting report. Maryland moved its walk-through — a session where coaches typically review opponents' tendencies and go through anticipated offensive and defensive sets at half speed — to the Marriott parking lot.

When Frese, getting up for the first time all day, emerged from the hotel elevator, she saw healthy players sitting on a couch in the lobby. Attempting to put her team at ease, she made a joke about the illness not being that bad. Toliver's shoulders were slumped as she arrived for the walk-through, and Walz was bedridden in his room. Frese assured Toliver they would both be fine, but everyone watched the clock as the game approached and silently prayed no one else became sick.

The No. 2 seed in the Albuquerque Region, Maryland traveled 1,900 miles to New Mexico's largest city in hopes of advancing to Boston. Utah, a good but not great team, was the region's fifth seed and the final obstacle between the Terps and a trip to Beantown. The Utes, led by four-time Mountain West Conference Player of the Year Kim Smith, were dangerous. Anchored by three senior starters, Utah had won 101 games and been to the tournament in three of the last four seasons, but this was the program's first Elite Eight appearance.

Coach Elaine Elliot's Utes were well-schooled in the motion offense, a system that allows players to read opposing defenses and make decisions based on what they see. It's an offense that works best with intelligent, experienced players — traits the Utes had in abundance. In addition to the 6-1 Smith, who averaged 19 points and 8 rebounds, Utah also featured Shona Thorburn, a 5-10 guard who averaged 12 points, 7.2 assists and 6.5 rebounds. Both were eventual first-round selections in the 2006 WNBA Draft and gave the Utes a chance against anyone on the schedule.

The Maryland-Utah clash pitted two teams that couldn't have been more different. Frese and the Terps, located just minutes from the nation's capital, were young, athletic and seemed to have the world at their feet. Conversely, Salt Lake City enjoys few of D.C.'s trappings while Elliot, owner of 490 career victories in 22 seasons as a head coach, and the Utes had strived for years for this rare chance. The only thing the two teams had in common was a desperate hunger to reach the Final Four.

When the Terps arrived at The Pit, they were far from 100 percent, but the team's greatest fear was of other players getting sick before or during the game.

Harper, Perry and Carr went through warm-ups, the severe stomach problems mostly gone. Their biggest concern was having the strength to perform at the requisite level in Albuquerque's thin air. Toliver was a different story. She literally rolled out of bed and onto the team bus. With her stomach still queasy, Toliver eschewed the normal pregame routine, choosing instead to conserve energy.

As Toliver sat on the bench watching her teammates warm up, Bernabei told her about playing one of her best games while battling the flu. As a player at West Liberty State College, a small Division II school in West Virginia's northern panhandle, Bernabei had scored more than 20 points and led the Hilltoppers to a come-from-behind win. She left the court only to discard the contents of her stomach. "Because you are sick, all the pressure is off you, so just go out there and play," Bernabei told Toliver. "If you've got to throw up, we will call a timeout and you can just run up the ramp and throw up and you will feel better and you can come back and play. It will be OK. You will have a lot of time after this game to feel sick. You've only a couple of hours to make the best of this, because this is our chance to go to the Final Four."

In the locker room before the game, talk among the players didn't center on how bad they felt at the moment but how bad they would feel after the game if their season ended one game short of the Final Four. Before Maryland took the floor the final message on its locker room chalkboard made no reference to the Final Four or Utah. It said, simply: "40 minutes of our will."

As the Terps walked down the ramp to enter the floor at The Pit, Frese saved a couple of words for Toliver, "She had grown up in the NBA and her idol was Michael Jordan," Frese said. "I told her, 'Do you remember MJ's greatest performance?' She just smirked, and I said, 'Let's go play.'" Frese was referring to Jordan's legendary 38-point performance in Game 5 of the 1997 NBA Finals. Battling dehydration and exhaustion as a result of the flu, Jordan led the Chicago Bulls back from a 16-point deficit to beat the Utah Jazz 90-88 en route to a 4-2 series victory.

In the game's opening minutes, Maryland played like a sick team, falling behind 6-1, but the Terps maintained their composure and used an 11-2 run, on the strength of three three-pointers, including one by Toliver, to take a 12-8 lead. But that torrid stretch of three-point shooting was the offensive highlight for Maryland in the first half. Whether it was because of nerves, illness or good defense by Utah, Maryland was otherwise unable to find its offensive rhythm. The Terps, who led the nation in three-point shooting at 40 percent, made only 4 of 14 attempts in the first half. Utah, leery of suffering the same fate as Baylor, double-teamed Langhorne every time she got the ball. Harper wasn't able to establish a consistent offensive threat in the first half, and the Utes turned Maryland into a perimeter team. Despite their accuracy from beyond the arc, the Maryland offense starts in the post, and Langhorne had just four points on two shots while Maryland converted a paltry 37.9 percent from the field in the first half.

With her team languishing on the offensive end, Frese, bedridden just 12 hours earlier, counseled, cajoled and implored her players throughout. In the hot, dry Albuquerque air, she actually sweated through her shirt as the virus continued to work its way out of her body, but she hid her struggles, attempting to show the type of energy she needed from her team on the court.

Playing an opponent it had never seen before, against an offense designed to carve up undisciplined defenses, Maryland turned in a stellar defensive effort, limiting Utah to 30.3 percent shooting and taking a 30-28 lead into the half. Smith, Utah's most prolific offensive player, was held scoreless in the opening 20 minutes, a feat that wouldn't be repeated in the second half.

The game's slow pace favored Utah, given that the more athletic Terps typically preferred an up-tempo game, but Frese didn't think her charges had enough energy to play at their normal breakneck pace. But the pace picked up in the opening minutes of the second half. With the Terps leading 34-28, Smith, who had missed her first six shots, took charge for Utah. She scored the game's next eight points, including consecutive three-pointers, to give the Utes a 36-34 lead, and suddenly the crowd at The Pit was roaring.

Albuquerque is the home of the University of New Mexico, a fierce rival of Utah, and one of the game's unknowns revolved around whether the local crowd would support the Utes. As Smith led the Utah charge, the crowd set aside its customary animosity to root for a Utah victory that could provide the MWC with a significant boost to its profile. Unlike most arenas, which have a semi-circle roof, the ceiling at The Pit was flat, a design that made it an exceedingly loud place to play. The building wasn't full, but the 6,823 spectators were making a lot of noise as Smith heated up.

After a basket by Langhorne tied the game, Smith resumed her heroics. Her three-pointers forced the Maryland defense to pressure the versatile forward on the perimeter, and she responded by driving for layups on Utah's next three possessions. Fortunately for the Terps, they had someone to counter every basket by Smith. Toliver, who had been sick in the parking lot during the walkthrough, started and revived memories of Jordan's 1997 performance — a game played, coincidentally, in Salt Lake City.

Toliver sandwiched a pair of three-pointers around a two-point basket to answer each Smith layup. A stretch of six possessions in which neither team missed a shot saw the Terps emerge with a 44-42 lead. Langhorne scored the next four Maryland points, pushing the lead to six before Smith answered with yet another basket. She scored Utah's first 16 points of the second half but didn't score again. Toliver answered Smith's final basket with another three-pointer, starting Maryland on a run of its own. With Toliver and Langhorne scoring at will, the Terps surged to a 56-47 lead capped by Toliver's sixth three-pointer of the game, a 22-footer from straight away.

"I was in a rhythm," Toliver said. "I don't even know what was going on in my head. I was just making them, so I figured I might as well take another one. I was just playing and not thinking." Toliver and Langhorne combined for 24 consecutive Maryland points. The run was a testament to the duo's individual skill, but it was out of character for the Terps. All five Maryland starters averaged in double figures throughout the season and the team's greatest strength was its multitude of scorers.

The Terps appeared poised to put Utah away, but nobody told the

Utes. Utah drained a couple of three-pointers to cut into the nine-point
deficit, and Maryland's offense suddenly stagnated. Toliver was visibly
wearing down, coughing on the floor, and her smooth jumper started
coming up short. Langhorne's layup pushed the Terps' lead back to 61-
54 with 6:54 remaining, but Maryland missed 12 of its final 13 shots, the
only exception being a jumper by Toliver at the 3:04 mark that increased
the lead to 63-58 before Utah's Morgan Warburton scored on consecutive possessions to bring the Utes within one with 1:55 remaining. Both
teams sputtered down the stretch, but after Coleman missed a jumper
with 31 seconds remaining, Utah, trailing 63-62, snared the rebound and
had a chance to pull the upset.

Elliot called a timeout and diagrammed a play that had Thorburn
driving the center of the lane and Newman, Maryland's best perimeter
defender, was whistled for a blocking foul with seven seconds remaining. Thorburn, a 73.6 percent foul shooter, was 4-for-4 from the line over
the last six minutes, and now the senior had a chance to give Utah the
lead and a likely victory.

The instant the whistle blew, a Maryland squad that had played with
the carefree attitude of an AAU team competing in a summer tournament, felt fear. A season the team was convinced would end in glory in
Boston was potentially two free throws from extinction. As Thorburn
toed the line, Toliver said more Hail Marys than she could count, and her
prayers were answered. Thorburn's first free throw hit off the back of
rim, bounced in the air and hit the front of the rim before falling out of
the cylinder. A palpable sense of relief came over the Maryland bench
before Thorburn made the second free throw, tying the game. Toliver
raced up court with the inbounds pass and hoisted up a running, one-
handed three-pointer that was off the mark. Doron picked up the
rebound, drew contact with a Utes defender and heaved a shot as the
horn sounded. Doron's shot missed and the Maryland bench howled for
a foul call that wasn't coming, but it was almost irrelevant.

"When she missed, I was like, 'The Gods are upon us,'" Bernabei
said of the first free throw. "They have been against us on this whole trip
[and they owed us one]. Going into overtime, we knew we were going
to win."

The no-call on Doron's shot was quickly forgotten because the
Terps were grateful to have five more minutes. For the fifth time in their
last 22 games, Maryland was heading into overtime. It had emerged
from the first four extra sessions unbeaten, making the Terps supremely
confident this game would be no different. "You could feel the energy
lift on the bench," Frese said of the missed free throw. "You are given a

second chance when you go into overtime. For our team, it probably took some of the nerves off. We didn't get it done in regulation, but we knew if we got some stops, we had a chance to win the game."

Maryland's 63 points in regulation represented its second-lowest 40-minute output of the season. Asking the Utah defense to hold the Terps in check for five minutes was a little too much. Maryland won the tap in overtime, fed the ball to Langhorne in the left high post and she hit Harper going to the basket for a layup 20 seconds into the extra session. Harper, who had six of her eight points in overtime, scored on the next possession, and the Terps never looked back. Maryland scored on six of its eight overtime possessions, and the defense forced the Utes to miss all seven of their field goal attempts. A season that seemed on the verge of ending minutes earlier had new life as the final horn sounded on a 75-65 Maryland victory. Toliver scored a career-high 28 points in a heroic effort, and the win touched off a Maryland celebration, replete with chest bumps, hugs and the cutting of the nets for a tired, but jubilant team.

"It was our heart [that won the game]," said Frese after the game, smiling but still under the weather. "They really grinded through it. We worked so hard for each other and found a way. Every X factor was against us in this game, and at times you can let your mind go in different directions to give yourself an excuse, but this team wouldn't let it. They really willed themselves to victory."

The Maryland Terrapins, led by Langhorne, the region's most outstanding player, were on their way to the Final Four for the first time since 1989.

After cutting down the nets and fulfilling their media obligations, the Terps, who were greeted by a rousing ovation in the hotel lobby from supporters who weren't sick, celebrated the big win. Unfortunately, Frese didn't have that option. During the game, her father, 74-year-old Bill Frese, fell ill. The man who had spent countless hours hauling her to youth league tournaments across the country when she was a child was forced to watch his daughter's finest hour while doubled over a trash can in the throes of the stomach virus that had nearly crippled her team.

Back at the hotel, Bill Frese's heart rate accelerated and he was

taken to the emergency room, where he was given fluid intravenously
and his heart rate was controlled. One of the longest and most fulfilling
nights of Brenda Frese's professional career ended at 3:30 a.m., with the
knowledge that her father was on the mend and the dream she promised
her players on the recruiting trail was on the brink of coming true.

Chapter 15

Final Four

M any factors had led Frese to accept the Maryland job nearly four years earlier. Not the least was Yow, someone Frese sensed from the outset shared her competitiveness.

In a meeting with all of Maryland's head coaches shortly after Frese joined the Terps, Yow said they all had the ability to be in the top 10. The AD knew every team wasn't going to be there at the same time, but she had understandably high expectations for the program. Frese loved it. Instead of running from expectations, she embraced them because it meant people were paying attention.

When the Maryland men's basketball team won the NCAA Tournament in 2002, the athletic department purchased the Georgia Dome floor the Final Four was played on and hung it in the Comcast Center. The sparkling national championship trophy was prominently displayed at the main entrance for fans to see on their way to games. The trophy display featured photos of team members and was a memorable tribute to a special team.

Displaying the confidence that has defined her rise, Frese initially asked Yow if she planned to erect a similar tribute when her team won a national title. Yow's answer was as quick as it was decisive: yes, the floor would be purchased and the trophy case installed when Frese and the Terps won a national title.

––––––––––

Frese was talking to her team in the locker room, walking the players through the Final Four schedule and trying to prepare them for what was coming. After concluding, she told the players to follow her from the locker room to the freight elevator.

Her players started to chatter: "What is Coach B going to do?" Several players guessed correctly that they were going to see the men's trophy. The short trip upstairs was a light one. Frese wanted her players to have a good time, but she had a serious message for them. She told her team to take a good look at the men's trophy and the pictures of players on the Comcast Center's Wall of Fame. Frese told her players their excitement about going to the Final Four was natural, but they shouldn't make the mistake of being satisfied.

"We have bigger goals than [just getting to the Final Four]," she told them. "Our goal is to be able to bring home a national championship trophy to be housed in a case like the men's. When ours is here, you are going to be able to bring back your families, your husbands and your kids and show them this trophy that will never be taken out of here."

The weary Terps returned from Albuquerque on the afternoon of Tuesday, March 28, the day after their win against the Utes, and they weren't finished with the virus that nearly helped end their season against Utah. Noirez, Coleman and Floyd got sick after Maryland returned home, but the Terps didn't play until Sunday, so all three had time to recover.

Maryland was going to Boston on Thursday, so its time was limited but the demands were not. Everyone's phone was ringing and media requests were mounting. The Terps had hardly been home since the tournament started two weeks earlier and now they had just 48 hours before leaving again. Frese encouraged players to rest and hydrate their bodies after the struggles in Albuquerque. Meanwhile, she cleared time for a massage for herself in an effort to relax.

Frese opened the team's Thursday practice to the public and the media to help prepare her team for the atmosphere surrounding the Final Four, and the school had a pep rally. There was a buzz in College Park about the team's run, but the players and coaches were so consumed with regaining their health and preparing for their third extended trip in as many weeks that time was a blur.

When the Terps arrived in Boston, sans Noirez who was too sick to travel with the team, they quickly realized how different the Final Four was when they had a police escort from Logan Airport to their hotel. The Maryland players bought into Frese's dream of creating their own legacy as opposed to building on someone else's. Between the trip to see the men's trophy case and the police escort to their hotel, the magnitude of what they were trying to do became increasingly clear.

Though the trappings surrounding the Final Four were different, the Terps saw a lot of familiar faces. The ACC was the strongest league in the country in the regular season, and its strength was borne out again in the tournament. North Carolina, Maryland's semifinal opponent, and Duke joined the Terps in the Final Four, making LSU the only non-ACC participant. The familiarity was probably a good thing for the Terps because it increased their comfort level. Thanks to Frese's early January trip, the players had already been to TD Banknorth Garden — they referred to it as their homecourt advantage — and their meeting with the Tar Heels would be the third in less than two months.

In keeping with a Final Four tradition, each team opened its practice, and several thousand people came for Maryland's. It was a different phenomenon for both players and coaches. The players were used to having people watch them perform — it's part of the allure of athletics — but people rarely watched them prepare. The fact so many people were in attendance illustrated the visibility and uniqueness of the Final Four.

From the perspective of Maryland's coaches, the feeling was similar. The Final Four, in addition to crowning a national champion, is a celebration of the game, and a host of events leading up to the games attract the vast majority of Division I head and assistant coaches. Coaches are basketball junkies, always looking for the opportunity to learn something new, which means a large number of them flock to the open practices. Frese and the members of her staff always used to do the same but now they were the ones being observed.

Frese joked with her assistants about bringing their "A" game with everybody watching, but her goal was to keep everyone loose. She emphasized not being happy with just getting to the Final Four, but she didn't want her team to get overwhelmed by the moment. The players played knockout, an old game where the objective is to make a shot from the free throw line before the person in front of you, therefore knocking that person out of the game, and kept things light. But Harper, the player whom drama seems to follow, experienced a little more. The players were doing some light running when Harper, who apparently didn't eat breakfast, fainted. "We were like, 'What are you doing?' " Langhorne said. "It was like she was asleep on the floor. I'm thinking in my head, because Harp is full of drama, 'You need to get up.' "

Langhorne and her teammates quickly realized she wasn't pretending to be asleep, but Harper was fine, much to everyone's relief. A temporarily scary situation quickly became something to laugh about, and fortunately for Harper, the images of her collapse weren't sent around the world. In addition to the "Under The Shell" cameras, a much higher profile group of videographers was chronicling the team in Boston. Frese agreed to allow ESPN to record their every move for an "All-Access" segment on the television network. Most coaches place restrictions on when and where the filming can take place, but not Frese. When Natalia Ciccone, the team's media relations coordinator, told ESPN of the full range of access, its representatives were pleasantly surprised.

"That kind of access is great for our program," Frese said of the ESPN segment. "It's the biggest stage, and I want people to see what we are like. We want to let people know how much fun we have."

Fun wasn't something many teams felt when playing North Carolina. The Tar Heels had rolled into the national semifinals with a record of 33-1. North Carolina was the NCAA Tournament's top overall seed, and the reward was a trip to the Cleveland Region and the tournament's toughest draw. The Tar Heels were forced to play a true road game in the second round at Vanderbilt, and Tennessee — a team that protested long and loud when it didn't get a No. 1 seed — was in the bottom half of their draw.

None of it mattered to the Tar Heels. North Carolina crunched Vanderbilt 89-70 in Nashville, setting up a Sweet 16 clash with Purdue. The talk of the tournament the day after the brackets were announced centered on the difficulty of North Carolina's draw, but the Boilermakers weren't expected to be its toughest challenge. Purdue played the Tar Heels to the wire but Ivory Latta, the ACC and national player of the year, made a layup with two seconds remaining to push UNC into the Elite Eight with a 70-68 victory.

In the region championship, North Carolina dismantled Tennessee 75-63 in a game that was never in doubt. The Lady Vols, the No. 1 team in the country entering the season, never led and were never closer than six points in the game's final 30 minutes. Led by Latta and Erlana Larkins, the Tar Heels were the nation's most feared team. North Carolina relied on a 1-3-1 trapping defense and often overwhelmed opponents by forcing turnovers in bunches and converting them into easy baskets.

The always expressive Latta, who never met a camera she didn't like, was the Tar Heels' leader from the point guard position. She averaged 18.4 points and 5.1 assists per game, but like her idol, Allen Iverson, she wasn't a classic point guard. Latta, charitably listed at 5-6, was jet quick, and always looking for her shot — she hoisted 137 shots more than anybody else on her team. Like the Philadelphia 76ers in Iverson's prime, North Carolina coach Sylvia Hatchell had a team that complemented Latta's game. Larkins and Little provided a physical presence in the paint and helped clear the way for Latta's frequent forays to the basket. When Latta was shooting the ball well, North Carolina was nearly impossible to beat, but she shared one less flattering trait with Iverson — there wasn't often a backup plan. She was going to take her shots, whether they were falling or not, and she could be frustrated.

As dynamic as Latta was, containing her wasn't No. 1 on Maryland's priority list. The Terps were the best rebounding team in the nation, grabbing 11.9 more per game than opponents, but in the ACC Tournament championship game North Carolina outrebounded them 48-37. If Maryland was going to beat the Tar Heels, it had to control the boards, and Frese wasn't going to let her team forget it.

Before the Terps left for Boston, the staff hung signs with the word "rebound" written in big, bold type. The signs were in the locker room, meeting rooms and even on the back of the bathroom doors. The signs went with the team to Boston as well.

As part of ESPN's "All-Access" segment, the network played a clip of Frese telling her players North Carolina was the team that needed to be worried. It sounded like typical coaching rhetoric, but in this case the Terps believed it. North Carolina was a heavy favorite, but Maryland had played well against Carolina in recent years, beating the Tar Heels by 15 at home the year before. Even in Frese's first season, the Heels narrowly avoided what would have been a shocking upset when they escaped College Park with an 83-82 victory.

While it seemed ridiculous on its face, Maryland was comfortable seeing North Carolina on the other side of the court. The Terps understood the intensity of the Tar Heels' trapping defense, but they thought Toliver could get the ball to the middle of the court and allow them to attack the 1-3-1.

The Terps, who played Hangman in the locker room during the tournament to kill time, tried not to approach the game as if it were the national semifinal. Aided by the fact Maryland was playing a familiar opponent in an arena it had visited early in the year, the players were telling themselves the Final Four was another chance at the ACC Tournament title.

As a team, Maryland entered the North Carolina game riding a wave of confidence, but Frese wanted to make sure Doron felt good about the state of her game. The most recognizable Terrapin had battled a thumb injury all season and was struggling. She made just 3 of 23 shots against St. John's, Baylor and Utah and totaled 19 points. After a game-day film session, Frese talked with Doron and brought the Maryland media guide along for the chat. Frese proceeded to read Doron's list of "noteworthy" accomplishments.

"Look at all the things you have accomplished," Frese said. "We are here because of you and the things you sacrificed for this team. You've done everything we've expected. But you are a great player, and we need you to play to the best of your abilities and play like the confident Shay."

There were 18,642 people in TD Banknorth Garden, and when the ball went in the air to start the first national semifinal, they gained an early look at Maryland's most trusted offensive weapon. Langhorne scored seven of the team's first 11 points, making three layups and getting the Terps off to a good start. Due to its experience playing against North Carolina's 1-3-1 trap, the Maryland staff believed its team would have the opportunity for easy buckets when not turning the ball over, and they were correct.

Maryland and North Carolina were two of the nation's three highest-scoring teams, and the game was played at a pace that would make a NASCAR driver proud. But the expected shootout didn't materialize in the first half. After Langhorne's three-point play gave the Terps an 11-8 lead less then four minutes into the game, they began giving up the ball at a staggering rate.

Maryland turned the ball over on six of its next nine possessions, sometimes because of good North Carolina defense and other times because of sloppy ball handling. To further complicate matters, the Tar Heels controlled the boards in the game's opening minutes, grabbing six offensive rebounds in their first 13 possessions. Though the Terps gave the ball away like Halloween candy and North Carolina was getting second-shot opportunities, the scoreboard didn't reflect Maryland's struggles.

The score was tied 18-18 when the Terps' spasm of six turnovers in nine possessions ended. Maryland was able to prevent North Carolina from opening a lead because when it didn't turn the ball over, it was shooting layups. The Terps scored on their first 12 possessions that didn't end in a turnover. Meanwhile, the Tar Heels were experiencing offensive troubles of their own.

With 12:24 to go in the half, Latta crumpled in pain after jamming her knee and had to be carried off the court by two teammates with the television cameras following the unfolding drama every step of the way. Fortunately for the Tar Heels, what appeared to be a serious injury passed. She returned to the game just 99 seconds later.

North Carolina's larger concern was the defensive job Maryland was doing on Latta. The Tar Heels liked to set screens for Latta at the top of the key, which often gave her enough space to attack the basket and create for herself or her teammates. But the Terps were doubling her off the screen, forcing Latta into a reactionary mode. Maryland's turnovers were worrisome but, almost amazingly, weren't leading to points for North Carolina. Instead of getting easy baskets in transition, the Tar Heels too often launched ill-advised three-pointers that didn't find their mark. Meanwhile, Maryland continued to pound the ball inside. The Terps didn't make their first shot from outside the paint until a jumper by Toliver gave them a 36-30 lead with 3:11 left in the half. Maryland, led by Langhorne's 7-for-8 shooting from the field and 15 points, took a 36-34 lead into the half despite committing 14 turnovers.

At the intermission, Maryland was the team full of confidence. Though they expected to win, the Terps didn't bear the pressure of everyone else's expectations, and they were looking forward to 20 more minutes with the Tar Heels.

The Terps endured an overabundance of turnovers in the second half as well, but when they got into their halfcourt offense, they were lethal. Instead of the up-tempo game expected, the contest turned into a battle of wills. It was physical, with each team giving as good as it got. Appropriately, one the game's key plays involved strength as opposed to flash.

With the Terps leading 54-48 and just under 10 minutes remaining, North Carolina turned it over, leaving Newman with the responsibility of bringing the ball upcourt. A natural shooting guard, Newman was hounded all the way by the Tar Heels' Alex Miller. Seeing that Newman was struggling against the pressure, Coleman came up to set a screen, and nobody bothered to tell the 5-6 Miller she was getting ready to run into Coleman. Miller hit Coleman on the run and dropped to the court with a thud. While Miller picked herself up off the floor, the Terps had a 5-on-4 advantage, and Coleman ended up getting fouled and going to the free throw line. Coleman's pick was clean and hard — Terps football coach Ralph Friedgen would have been proud — and it energized the crowd and in turn, Maryland. North Carolina physically intimidated a lot of teams through the season, but the Terps weren't going to be one of them.

Coleman was fouled late in the game and made both free throws, and the Terps were in a run that pushed their lead to 63-52. While Maryland's confidence seemed to grow with each made basket, North Carolina began to sag. Maryland was in control throughout the second half, but North Carolina made a late charge. The Tar Heels scored on three consecutive possessions to cut the Maryland lead to 70-68, as close as they had been since the 15:22 mark of the second half. Doron, an 82.8 percent free throw shooter, was fouled on the Terps' next possession. With 1:58 remaining, Doron had three points on 1 of 4 shooting and missed the first free throw.

In a game Maryland had seemed to have a firm grasp, Doron's second shot suddenly carried additional weight. A miss and North Carolina could tie or take the lead on its next trip down the court. But Doron made the free throw, and Larkins missed a quick jumper at the other end. Coleman grabbed the rebound and threw the outlet pass to Doron, who pressed the attack before making a jumper in the lane, pushing the Maryland lead to five.

Latta made a pair of free throws to cut the Maryland lead to 73-70 with 1:06 remaining. Toliver had 12 of Maryland's 26 turnovers and, with the Terps desperately needing to protect the ball and get a good shot, Frese turned to Doron. Frese talked with her earlier in the day about the team's need for her to play big, and now the coach was entrusting her on one of the game's biggest possessions.

Doron took the inbounds pass and struggled against Latta's defense, but with the shot clock winding down, she turned the corner and broke free. Doron went straight for the basket and found Harper open along the baseline just a few feet from the bucket. Harper caught the ball and laid it in for the final two of her career-high 24 points. Maryland was up 75-70, and the result became a formality. The Terps hit six free throws down the stretch, the final two coming after Latta slammed Coleman to the floor a full second or two after the play had been whistled dead, to account for the 81-70 final score.

Maryland earned its first trip to the NCAA Championship. Langhorne made 10 of 12 shots and finished with 23 points, while Coleman had 12 points and, more importantly, 14 rebounds. The Terps placed an emphasis on rebounding and their domination of the boards proved to be one of the key differences. With 16:42 left in the game, Maryland had a narrow 24-23 edge on the boards and was trailing 42-40. The Terps outrebounded the Tar Heels 17-8 the rest of the way and outscored them by 13 points.

The Terps entered the Final Four with no expectations other than their own, and that may have accounted for the calm Frese felt. For whatever the reason, Frese was as relaxed as she had been all year at the Final Four, and her demeanor allowed the team to thrive. Coaches are like players — the bigger the situation, the more tense some get. And when a coach gets tense, the players sense it. Frese was doing just the opposite. The bigger the situation, the more relaxed she seemed to be. She got a little frustrated with the officiating early in the game, but she left it behind and told her team to do the same. Nothing illustrated her almost preternatural calm like the way she dealt with Toliver. Latta may have been struggling on the offensive end, but she hounded Toliver all over the court, and the freshman finished the game with 12 turnovers. Very little drives a coach as crazy as turnovers and 12 by the point guard is mind-numbing, but Frese never lost her cool with Toliver.

When the stakes were at their highest, Frese fell back on a lesson she had learned from coaching her sister, Stacy, at Iowa State: Players don't go on stage and try to perform badly. They want to succeed, but some nights it's more difficult than others. Frese stayed positive with her young point guard and was rewarded for her faith. Toliver struggled to handle the ball all night, but she scored nine of her 14 points in the final 14 minutes.

"Coach kept reinforcing, 'You are fine,' " Toliver said. "She definitely keeps you upbeat and stays positive all the time, and it helps a lot."

––––––––––––––––––

In the second semifinal, LSU played Duke, and there was little doubt in the minds of the Maryland players about who was going to win. They didn't think anybody playing Duke for the first time had much of a chance, and they were right. The Blue Devils cruised to a 64-45 victory, setting up an all-ACC national title game.

After fulfilling a host of media obligations and scouting the Duke-LSU game, the entire Maryland coaching staff and Ciccone called a cab to take them back to the team hotel. They went outside, but the cab went to the wrong side of the building. Frese, Walz, Pearson, Bernabei and Ciccone were standing on a Boston street corner, unable to hail a taxi. They waited for 30 minutes, staring at an event sign that said, "Then there were four."

Tired after a long day but too happy to be mad, Ciccone screamed, "Then there were two."

Standing anonymously on the street, the Terps' coaches laughed and waited for the second cab.

Chapter 16

"I Knew She was Going to Shoot the Ball"

The day after Maryland's victory over North Carolina was the fourth anniversary of Frese's introductory press conference at Maryland, and now she was again facing the media. Instead of talking to local reporters covering the team, Frese was addressing a throng from across the country, and the press conference was carried live on ESPN News. The ascension of the Maryland program had been stunningly swift, and the Terps were one win away from capturing the national title that motivated Frese to take the Maryland job.

Standing between the Terps and what the players believed to be their destiny was Duke. Maryland had measured itself against the Blue Devils, often falling short in a series of humbling losses. The 101-52 loss to Duke in January 2003 still ranked as the nadir of Frese's coaching career — the only time she doubted, even briefly, whether Maryland could reach that level. But just as Yow predicted after that game, things had changed dramatically.

As the level of Maryland's play rose, Duke remained as the hurdle the Terps were unable to clear until the ACC Tournament. At the time, Maryland's semifinal victory against the Blue Devils was regarded as a big one, but it turned out to be more significant than anyone imagined. The victory lifted what the Maryland players called the monkey off their backs. With the biggest game of their career on the horizon, the Terps weren't forced to wrestle with internal demons. They knew they could beat Duke, even if they weren't expected to.

The pressure of the national championship game can be suffocating, and try as coaches might, it's difficult to pawn it off as just another game. The tournament itself is a different animal because of travel, unusual starting times for some games and the time spent in the arena doing nothing. It's difficult to carve out time for the players to see their family members who often have taken vacation days to come see them play on the game's biggest stage. With that in mind, Frese eschewed the typical team meal the night before the game and let her players eat with their families. Moments like the one Maryland was experiencing are rare, and Frese wanted the players to be able to share it. She had a host of family in Boston, as well. Four of her five siblings, including Marsha and Stacy, were at the Final Four, along with her parents and a slew of nieces and nephews. The Frese family invested a lot time and emotion into the game of basketball, and they enjoyed seeing one of their own within a step of the mountaintop.

Maryland was loose on the day of the championship game, joking at breakfast. All season long, the Terps believed they were fighting a losing battle for respect in the insular world of women's college basketball, and Frese had been given a final bit of ammunition for the no-respect cannon she had been firing.

The day after Maryland's semifinal win against North Carolina, Sally Jenkins' column in the Washington Post painted a less-than-flattering picture of the Terps effort in the win. Jenkins, a Tar Heel alum and author of two books with Summitt, called the game "savagely played, brutally coached and badly officiated." She was right on one account: It was a physical game. But Jenkins offered no evidence to support her thoughts about the quality of the coaching. Jenkins made reference to Frese sneering and shrieking at officials, called the Maryland uniforms ugly and stopped just short of calling the Terps a dirty team.

In the eyes of the Maryland faithful, the column was unbecoming for a paper of the Washington Post's stature. It appeared a petty attack, something that was difficult to figure given Jenkins had never talked to Frese. Whatever the cause, Frese had the article copied and gave it to her players the day of the championship game and told them one more win was obviously needed to gain the respect of even their hometown newspaper.

North Carolina had entered the tournament as the favorite, but Duke had plenty of supporters. The Blue Devils, with the exception of a 63-61 overtime win against Connecticut in the Bridgeport Region final, clobbered their opposition in the tournament. Duke beat Southern by 69 points in the opening round, Southern California by 34 in the second and Michigan State by 25 in the Sweet 16. After dominating LSU in the second semifinal in Boston, many people felt Goestenkors and Duke were ready to claim their first national title.

An already imposing Duke team had become even more so with the emergence of 6-7 Alison Bales in the tournament. Bales averaged 9.1 points and 6.7 rebounds during the season, but she was dominant at times during the NCAAs, particularly in her 15-point, 13-rebound effort against Connecticut. With Bales playing at such a high level in conjunction with Currie, Harding and the rest of her teammates, Duke would be very difficult to beat.

Duke was well-coached, executed with ruthless precision, and offered no surprises. Maryland had one significant factor working in its favor: familiarity with the Blue Devils. Duke was very skilled on the perimeter. Harding, Currie and Wanisha Smith, were threats from three-point range. With Bales and Mistie Williams — the 6-3 daughter of singer Chubby Checker — it had tremendous size on the interior. Without having played against Duke's size and all-around skill, it is difficult for teams to prepare, hence Doron's confidence the Blue Devils would beat LSU in the semifinals.

Maryland had no such issue. The championship game was the fourth meeting between the two teams in less than three months. The Terps knew when and where the Duke double teams would be coming from, and with each game they learned to better counteract the Blue Devils' size.

"It was a huge advantage for us because we could say this is what I need to do to be successful against [Bales]," Walz said. "That was a big plus for us. We worked on facing up to the basket instead of trying a turnaround jumper over [an opponent who was] 6-7. We worked on getting to the other side of the rim, using the rim as a deterrent."

———————————

There were no scouting report gimmicks because no matter how large Duke loomed on the Terps' schedule, the national title game was much bigger than the Blue Devils. Frese didn't deliver a speech focusing just on the national title and what it would mean, choosing instead to focus on the journey her players had traveled and the fun she wanted them to have in the locker room before the game.

Each day when the team bus pulled into TD Banknorth Garden, the driver was forced to back into a narrow ramp, a feat that amazed the team. They wouldn't have felt comfortable backing a car up the ramp, much less a bus. Frese talked to her team about the similarities between what the driver did and their season. The driver had to have skill and confidence to maneuver the bus through a narrow passage with little margin for error on either side, just as the Terps had all season. The road to the national championship game is perilous, and Frese told her team it had persevered through difficult times, particularly in Albuquerque, all for the reward of playing on that night. As she did throughout the season, Frese told her team how she envisioned the game unfolding.

"We are going to go out for the best 40 minutes of your life," Frese recalled saying. "I talked about how as the game unfolded we were going to get stronger as a team, like we did in the season. By the time we got to the second half, everyone was going to see a team getting stronger and stronger. We are going to keep running the lane and rebounding so hard Duke is going to look around and say, 'What happened?' "

And, Frese told her team, "You aren't going to want this game and this stage to end. You are going to want to keep playing to show how special you are."

There are many reasons, beyond winning, why Frese has become such a popular figure in College Park and has inspired great loyalty from her staff. Frese never fails to credit the people who helped her achieve success. When Walz makes a good call in the huddle, Frese issues private and public praise after the game. She doesn't have an ego that prevents others from getting the credit, and Langhorne's basket at the end of the first half of the Baylor game was a prime example. Walz saw something, called for a change in the play and the Terps scored a crucial basket as the buzzer sounded. Frese made sure everyone knew Walz was responsible for the call after the game.

A couple of years earlier, Charvat, the team's trainer since Frese had arrived, was on the verge of accepting a job at another university and told Frese he was likely leaving. Frese's first question was, what can we do to keep you? Frese then went to bat with the athletic department for Charvat, who remained on the Maryland staff. The job of a trainer can be thankless and the hours are long, but it's a vital position. The trainer helps injured athletes heal, and the work of Charvat and Rooks was vital to the team's efforts to recover from the illnesses against Utah.

With Maryland and Duke getting lined up for the national anthem minutes before the biggest game of their lives, Frese put her arm around Charvat's shoulders and told him she was happy he was with the team. Win or lose, gestures like that one are the reason for Frese's popularity in College Park.

Maryland trotted out the youngest lineup in NCAA championship game history: one junior, two sophomores and two freshmen. The question surrounding the Terps all year had been whether a team so young could advance as far as their talent suggested. The answer was a resounding yes, but Maryland looked young in the first half against Duke. The Blue Devils made stopping Langhorne the focal point of their defense and were successful, limiting her to four points on just one field goal attempt in the first half. Each time Langhorne touched the ball, there were at least two Duke defenders hovering and sometimes three.

Though Langhorne tossed a couple of post-to-post passes to Harper that led to easy scores, she was largely neutralized. Duke sold out to stop Langhorne, and the Terps were unable to make them pay. The Blue Devils had offensive problems of their own, missing numerous layups in the opening minutes before finally finding a bit of a rhythm.

Defensively, the Terps made the decision not to double-team Bales, choosing instead to focus on Currie and Harding, both of whom had given the Terps fits in the first three meetings. Unfortunately, all three had big first halves, particularly Harding, who scored 13 points in the opening 20 minutes. After Currie made a layup and was fouled, she converted the free throw to give Duke a 34-21 lead with 4:21 left in the half, and the Terps were in trouble. The Blue Devils had chances to increase their lead, thanks at least in part to a couple of turnovers by Coleman, who, like Toliver, was struggling to control her nerves and her emotions. If Maryland was to have any chance, Coleman needed to be productive, and Frese wanted to make sure she knew it.

With 2:36 remaining, the horn blew for the final media timeout of the half, and Frese went directly for Coleman, meeting her on the floor. Frese put a hand on each side of Coleman's midsection, looked directly into her eyes and started telling her in a very animated tone what was expected of her. Coleman occasionally tried to look away, but Frese brought her back each time. The conversation was one-sided and full of passion as Frese's head bobbed with emotion — the assumption being that she was lambasting her rising star for her poor performance.

"It looked like I had just had a turnover and I was getting yelled at," Coleman said. "Coach B knows how to motivate me, getting in my face with a lot of energy. She didn't say one negative thing to me that whole time. She said, 'You are too good a player to be in this kind of funk. You aren't having fun. You are playing the game you love. In order for us to win this game, we need you. You need to get your head in the game. You are going to hit big shots for us, and we are going to be cutting down the nets.' "

Coleman wasn't the only Terp who wasn't having a lot of fun in the first half. Newman, sitting on the bench with two fouls, nearly had tears in her eyes as she watched her team struggle and begged to be put back in the game. With 1:38 to go in the half and Maryland trailing 38-25, Frese reinserted Newman, and two possessions later she buried a three-pointer to make the score 38-28, at the break.

Coaches are forced to make decisions everyday, some large, some small, some that have an impact never imagined when they are made. After the North Carolina game, Frese needed to choose a locker room. Maryland could stay in the locker room used against North Carolina, which would put them across the hall from the Blue Devils and force the Terps to walk an extra distance to their bench. The other choice was the locker room North Carolina had used that was closer to Maryland's bench. The Terps weren't a superstitious team so Frese selected the locker room closest to their bench. When the Maryland players were taken to it, they howled in protest, saying they didn't want to use the losers' locker room. Figuring she should pick her battles wisely, Frese asked to return to the original locker room, and the request was granted.

As the Terrapins returned to their locker room at the half, they listened to Duke celebrating. But Maryland didn't have to hear the Blue Devils at the half to know they were feeling good about themselves. Perry, who wears size 15 men's shoes, was sporting a pair of Scottie Pippen model Nikes with "Air" written across them. At one point in the first half when the players were lined up along the lane waiting for a free throw attempt, Currie looked down at Perry's feet and said, "Damn, Jade, your feet are so big your shoes [read] 'A-I-I-I-I-R.' " The crack drew a laugh, even from Perry's teammates, and illustrated just how comfortable the Blue Devils were feeling.

Duke reveled in its 10-point lead, but Maryland, despite as ugly a first half as it played all season, found reason for quiet optimism. There was no yelling in frustration at the half or finger pointing. As Frese and her staff met in the hallway outside the locker room they could hear their players talking to each other. Langhorne told teammates each needed to play harder. Doron pointed out what they all felt was Duke's premature celebration. The development of internal leadership had been a focal point for the team since its first meeting on Sept. 1, more than seven months ago. In the biggest game of the year, Frese and her staff liked what they heard from their locker room before they ever stepped into it.

When Frese addressed the players, she didn't blister them. She was excited the Terps were only down 10 — a deficit they had overcome before. Frese did chastise them for their poor body language, reminding her team of the look it saw on North Carolina's face two nights earlier — a look that signaled defeat and how it filled Maryland with confidence.

Frese asked her players what they thought Duke saw when looking at the frustration etched on their faces in the first half. She said they were fortunate to have 20 minutes to turn around the game. As Frese questioned her team about its body language, Bernabei could see the message taking hold with Toliver, who had struggled through a game and a half in the Final Four.

Maryland headed back onto the floor, feeling as good as a team that had shot 32 percent and trailed by 10 points could possibly feel, but it didn't have much margin for error. The start of the second half looked a lot like the first, with the Terps struggling to score. Fortunately for Maryland, Duke turned the ball over on four of its first nine possessions and wasn't able to push its lead beyond 12.

The game changed at the 15:21 mark of the second half when Doron picked off Harding's pass and raced downcourt for a layup, cutting the deficit back to 10. After Doron made two free throws on Maryland's next possession, Langhorne stole Abby Waner's pass, went the length of the court and drew a foul on Harding. After Langhorne converted the free throw, Maryland trailed by just 45-37, and a team searching for a spark was suddenly full of life.

Coleman, who had struggled so badly in the opening half, was the best player on the court for a crucial stretch. She rebounded a miss by Bales, raced downcourt and pulled up for a 17-foot jumper to bring Maryland within 57-56 with 6:51 remaining. Coleman headed back down the court with her neck craned toward the arena's rafters, screaming with delight and throwing uppercuts at the air. A once-silent Maryland bench came alive. Less than a minute and a half later, Langhorne made 1 of 2 free throws, and the Terps had a 59-58 lead — their first since the opening minutes, but Duke quickly responded. After Bales hit two free throws to give Duke the lead, Currie scored six of the Blue Devils' next eight points, giving Duke a four-point edge it carried into the game's final minute.

Despite a miserable start, Maryland played a superb second half but still trailed 68-65 with 35 seconds to go and Waner at the free throw line for Duke. But Waner missed the front end of a one-and-one, and Toliver rushed the ball upcourt, made a spin move at the free throw line and hit a fadeaway jumper from 13 feet to bring the Terps within one.

Duke's Jessica Foley made a pair of free throws to push the Blue Devils' lead to 70-67 with 18.8 seconds left, but Maryland had one last opportunity to tie. After the Terps brought the ball to halfcourt, Frese called a timeout with 15.4 seconds remaining.

Moments earlier Frese had asked Walz to have a play prepared. The staff huddled and Walz recommended a maneuver that called for Toliver to pass the ball to Coleman at the top of the key, and then run off a screen that would free her up for what Maryland hoped would be a game-tying three-pointer in the right corner.

As Frese, Walz and Floyd wrapped up their discussion, Bernabei slipped out of the coaches' huddle and went to the bench to talk briefly with the Maryland players. With 15 seconds left, the Terps had plenty of time, and she told them to make sure they got their feet set and took a good shot. She then looked directly at Toliver and repeated, "Don't just throw up a shot, make it a good one."

In a big situation early in the year against Tennessee, Toliver passed up a potential game-winning shot, but the Maryland staff was confident it wouldn't happen again. She's not giving the ball up was the thought going through the minds of Floyd and Bernabei as the Terps headed onto the court for the biggest 15 seconds of their basketball lives.

On cue, Toliver took the inbounds from Coleman who went to the top of the key to set a screen and await a pass from Toliver, but the ball never came. Toliver raced around the right side of the arc and the heady Langhorne, seeing what was happening, stepped up to screen Toliver's defender, leaving the 6-7 Bales responsible for Toliver. A post player's instinct is to defend the drive when guarding a smaller player on the perimeter, and Bales hedged ever so slightly towards the basket, freeing up Toliver to get a clear look.

Toliver, a foot shorter than her defender, stepped back and with Bales running at her with her arms up, squeezed off a three-pointer from 21 feet. As she released the ball, Toliver felt Bales' hand brush hers, but Bales was too late in getting there. The Maryland bench rose to its feet, collectively thinking, "Damn, that looks good."

With 6.2 seconds remaining, the ball swished through the net. Toliver's outstretched arms went in the air signalling a "three," and she was nearly tackled by Harper and Perry, who were going crazy on the sideline. There were 18,642 spectators, most of them as fans of the game rather than necessarily Maryland or Duke, but when Toliver's shot went in, the building erupted, sending a jolt across the court none of the Maryland players will soon forget.

But now they had to defend for six more seconds. Harding took the inbounds pass and raced the length of the court, coming up short on a shot as the horn sounded. The national championship game was tied 70-70, and Maryland was going wild. Toliver was mugged on the Terps' bench, and a familiar scream echoed through the huddle:

"Overtime is our time!"

Never had a team been surer of victory than the Terps as they prepared for their sixth overtime game of the season.

––––––––––

In its earlier overtime games, Maryland rushed to an early lead, winning the tip and scoring early, but now the Terps, still buzzing from Toliver's shot, didn't immediately re-establish their offensive flow. Maryland failed to score in the first three minutes of overtime, but Duke, still stunned at what had happened at the end of regulation, turned the ball over on three of its first four possessions. When Doron made a pair of free throws with two minutes remaining, Maryland drew even 72-72.

The two teams then traded baskets, and Bales made one of two free throws to give the Blue Devils a 75-74 lead. On Maryland's next possession, Toliver drew Harding's fifth foul, forcing the Duke player out of the game. Toliver made both free throws to give Maryland a one-point lead with 34 seconds left. Waner then missed a jumper, and Coleman grabbed the rebound and was fouled with 13.4 seconds remaining and Maryland leading 76-75. The Blue Devils used their final timeout, hoping to ice Coleman and set up their own potential game-tying or even game-winning play, depending on the result of the free throws.

Frese kept things light in the huddle and emphasized the need for her team to defend after Coleman made both free throws. Coleman had morphed from struggling freshman in the first half into the game's best player in the final 15 minutes. She had made clutch shots, owned the boards and played solid defense on Currie. Now she had the opportunity to make a pair of free throws and push Maryland's lead to three.

Coleman walked onto the court with a smile, confident as ever, and gave Toliver a hug. The two had committed to Maryland together, even if Coleman had temporarily wavered, and a year earlier vowed to be playing in the 2006 Final Four. Toliver delivered one of the more dramatic shots in the event's 25-year history minutes earlier, and now her roommate had a chance to hit the title-clinching free throws.

"Make these free throws, and let's go cut the nets down," Toliver told Coleman. The trip to the line was Coleman's first of the game, but the 83.3 percent free throw shooter performed as if she were in an open gym. She nailed both, pushing the Maryland lead to 78-75.

With Harding fouled out, Waner had to take the ball upcourt for Duke, which still had 13.4 seconds left. Toliver hounded her all the way, forcing the Blue Devils to burn precious seconds while advancing the ball. Waner eventually passed to Jessica Foley, who heaved up a long three-pointer with just less than two seconds on the clock. The shot barely grazed the front of the rim, falling into Coleman hand's for her 14th rebound of the game.

Maryland 78, Duke 75.

The Maryland Terrapins were national champions in women's basketball for the first time in school history.

Doron, Langhorne, Toliver, Newman and Coleman, the five players on the court at the end of the game, raised their arms in the air and sprinted toward their teammates, meeting them, appropriately, at midcourt.

The Terps yelled, laughed, cried and hugged. Maryland, the team that was too young, had overcome the second-largest deficit in championship game history to beat a Duke squad that had tormented it like no other in its growth from a 10-18 squad four years ago to national champions.

In the stands, the Frese family, like those of the players, shed tears of joy. Basketball had been an integral part of their lives for decades, and now one of their own had reached its zenith. When they made it to the court, Frese's husband gave her a kiss on one cheek while her father kissed the other. The Terps cut the nets down for the second time in less than a week, but nobody was sick this time. There was only pure joy as each player, coach and administrator climbed the ladder to claim his or her piece of the prize they all dreamed of winning.

Perry shared an emotional embrace in the stands with her mother, who at one point feared she would never see her daughter play in a Maryland uniform because of her bout with cancer, and her sister Jasmine to whom she was so close. Her high school coach, whose mother had recently died, made the trip to see his former star as well.

Langhorne's parents, who never made basketball the priority in their house, were as emotionally involved in the game as any other parent, embracing the success of their daughter, who had grown into the game's most humble star.

George Toliver knew the game intimately, and his daughter, whose play seemed to parallel the team's through the year, had grown in a matter of months from being a struggling girl leaving home for the first time to a thriving young woman, in all aspects of her life.

Frese relentlessly sold her dream to each of her players, who had the strength to believe in the personality and vision of their young coach. It hadn't been easy for 16-and-17-year old girls to tell their peers they weren't going to Tennessee or UConn, but they had made a bold decision, and the rewards were sweeter than they could have even imagined.

Chapter 17

A Budding Super Power?

When the Terps returned to College Park the day after the championship game, they arrived to find a different atmosphere than before. Students, who had selectively embraced the team, showed up in droves at a pep rally to celebrate the national championship. The size of the crowd surprised the players and was the first indicator of how things were beginning to change for Frese and the team.

The young champions then were honored at the White House by President George W. Bush and at the Maryland State House by Gov. Robert Ehrlich. Frese, accompanied by her team, threw out the first pitch at a Baltimore Orioles game days later, and the Terps were feted by the NBA's Washington Wizards and the WNBA's Washington Mystics.

The most substantial, and in many ways rewarding changes, came in the recognition the players received from classmates and in public. A trip to the grocery store or a restaurant included saying hello to fans and signing a couple of autographs.

"It's been great all the recognition we've been getting," Coleman said. "People are asking for autographs and pictures. People you didn't think would be watching are saying thanks for the championship."

The nature of the team's tournament run — overcoming illness against Utah and battling back from a 13-point deficit against Duke, the school's biggest athletic rival — struck a chord with the Terps' faithful. In the immediate aftermath of the championship, Maryland more than doubled its season ticket sales for the 2006-07 season.

As much as Maryland's season was about the NCAA Tournament, what made the run possible was the players' belief in one another and the coaching staff. Team chemistry is elusive and difficult to quantify, but the 2005-06 Terps had a special togetherness. The public perception of a team is that of one big family, but in reality there are often fierce battles within a group for status and playing time. The Terps genuinely liked and rooted for one another. When Langhorne, an Associated Press All-America selection, was left off the more prestigious Kodak/WBCA All-American team, it was her teammates who were angry.

"I don't understand what the criteria for an all-American is," Harper said disgustedly. "But I know she has done everything for this team. I think she is the best center in the country. She is a leader, and she has put this team on her back countless times. I think that is what it takes to be an all-American."

The players bought into what Frese told them since the start. Perry and Newman believed in the "seven starters" concept that had them coming off the bench, a crucial part of the Terps' success. While Langhorne, Harper, Toliver, Doron and Coleman piled up gaudy numbers, Perry and Newman gave Maryland defensive toughness. Perry scored four points and grabbed two rebounds in the championship game against Duke — modest numbers, but if you asked the coaching staff and the players about the keys to the game, they will point without fail to Perry's defense against Bales. Duke's big center played an outstanding game, finishing with 19 points and 12 rebounds, but Perry provided the type of physical play that Langhorne and Harper, despite all their other gifts, could not. The Terps' camp believed Perry's presence helped fatigue Bales just enough to slow her down the stretch.

Newman hit numerous big shots. Some like the three-pointer to give Maryland the lead late in the second half against St. John's get lost in the blur of a season of highlights, but no matter the role, she always responded. The three-pointer she flung in at the buzzer to send the game at North Carolina into overtime was, in its own way, as big as Toliver's shot against Duke. From that point forward, Maryland believed it could win the national title.

Langhorne and Doron were the team's leaders and remained that way through the end. Langhorne is a brilliant player, a legitimate national player of the year candidate, and one the Terps could always count on for a basket. She was at her best when the games counted most, averaging 22 points during the NCAA Tournament while drawing constant double coverage, with the notable exception of the Baylor game.

The Final Four was as rewarding for Doron as anyone. No player on the team altered her role more than the junior. She led the Terps in scoring each of her first two years but sacrificed points and shots for the greater goal of winning. She led the team through action and words, playing point guard when necessary and helping Toliver through difficult times. Though her role as a scorer was reduced, Doron's attitude over three seasons was instrumental in changing the mindset of the program. Her play in the final two minutes against North Carolina in the national semifinals was pivotal. Her 16-point, four-steal performance against Duke in the title game was typical Doron as she sacrificed her body countless times in pursuit of the only goal, the championship Doron had been seeking since she was a freshman.

Maryland's ultimate success was closely linked with the development of Toliver, Coleman and Harper, the least experienced of the Terps who played significant minutes.

Toliver's evolution was in many ways the key to the team's tournament success, because by late March and early April, the freshman who had been struggling on the court and in the classroom was long gone. She wrote Frese a note saying she wanted to be a player the team could count on, and that is what Toliver became. She excelled in the classroom during the second semester, which made it easier for her to focus on the court. In January, Toliver fretted that no one knew who she was. By April 5, most sports fans had heard her name. The shot Toliver hit to send the championship game into overtime is arguably the second-most memorable in tournament history, ranking only behind the buzzer-beating jumper by North Carolina's Charlotte Jones that propelled the Tar Heels to a 60-59 win against Louisiana Tech in the 1994 title game.

"My game changed, and my attitude changed in practices and games," Toliver said. "When you are taking care of things academically, basketball is all you have to worry about. If you aren't ready for an exam you have tomorrow that is what you will be thinking about during practice. In the spring, my head was clear and I had everything together."

In some ways, Toliver bears little resemblance to the shy freshman who arrived on campus in the summer of 2005. She may never be the team's most loquacious player, but by the end of the season, she was at ease speaking with the media and even making public appearances. She gave a 20-minute talk at her father's officiating camp in Harrisonburg, Va., and Frese brought Toliver and Coleman along to speak to a leadership class on campus.

On the court, Toliver never lacked for confidence or shied away from the moment — something the shot against Duke made abundantly clear — but her gutsy performance against Utah said just as much about her competitive character.

Frese's late January meeting with Harper may have been the most important of the season. Langhorne's excellence was a given, but when

Harper elevated her game, teams were punished for the attention they heaped on Langhorne. As her confidence grew, so did Harper's play. She averaged 20 points and 8 rebounds in the Final Four and was named the event's most outstanding player. Though she was the first to acknowledge the award could have gone to several other players, the trophy was a sweet reward for Harper. She worked diligently to overcome the Achilles injury and to find her role on the team, and the player Frese recruited to be a star summoned her best basketball on the biggest stage.

Coleman is unique in women's basketball, and provided Maryland with the rarest of commodities, someone who played every position from point guard to power forward at a high level. She was the dominant player on the boards in the Final Four, grabbing 28 rebounds, the fourth-highest in the event's history. As good as Coleman was on the glass, her ability to create shots for herself was equally important against Duke. With size and ability to handle the ball, Coleman could pull up off the dribble and score like few players in the women's game, making ordinarily difficult shots look easy.

Maryland grew from a team as inexperienced as it was talented to a champion in six months. The credit for that development goes to the players who worked hard enough to make it happen, as well as to Frese and her staff. Frese worked from the day she walked on campus to create a positive environment for the team. That doesn't mean there isn't discipline or she doesn't scold them, because, like every coach, she does. What separates Frese is the fact she doesn't tear her players down when reprimanding them. The result of her message is nearly always positive, and the importance of that can't be overlooked on a team as young as the Terrapins.

"That's what helped us win a championship. You see Coach B standing on the sideline with her arms crossed going, 'You are OK [even during difficult times],' " Harper said. "She was always like, 'You will be fine. You will get the next one.' I've never seen anybody so positive."

That quality paid dividends from the recruiting trail to the Final Four. The Terps had complete faith in the direction provided by the coaching staff, and in turn, the staff, still young itself, had an unshakable belief that its players could pull out any game.

The faith that both sides had proved to be justified. The Terps finished the season 34-4, setting a school record for victories. Maryland lost to Tennessee, North Carolina and Duke twice. In three of the four losses, the opponent was ranked No. 1, the only exception being the loss to Duke at home when the Blue Devils were ranked No. 2. The Terrapins played 38 games against one of the nation's most difficult schedules and didn't suffer one bad loss.

In retrospect, each of their losses proved valuable. If Maryland had defeated Tennessee in the Virgin Islands, would the Terps have worked as hard to improve, thinking they were already a Final Four team? The home loss to Duke showed them what it took to be a Final Four team, and the loss in Durham was evidence of how close they were to being one. The setback against North Carolina in the ACC Tournament finals called attention to the team's need to rebound and be more physical in the NCAA Tournament games.

After years of dominance by Tennessee and UConn — teams that several Terps players spurned on the recruiting front — Maryland now has a chance to be the game's dominant team over the next several years. The Terps almost certainly will enter the 2006-07 season as the consensus preseason No. 1 team.

Buoyed by the confidence gained from her play over the season's final two months, Harper should combine with Langhorne and Perry to form one of the best frontcourts in the nation the next two years. In the backcourt, Doron returns for the final year of one of the most prolific careers in Maryland history. With their stellar play down the stretch, it's easy to forget that Coleman and Toliver were just freshmen. Typically, a player can expect to see considerable improvement from freshman to sophomore season, a frightening prospect for Terps opponents. Newman also returns as the team's best perimeter defender and a player with a knack for making big shots.

The Terps will return all "seven" starters and 98 percent of their point production and 95 percent of their rebounding. Staggering as those numbers are, the small percentage of production that isn't returning was mostly accumulated against overmatched teams. Maryland returns 100 percent of its offense from the final five games of the NCAA Tournament and 98 percent of its rebounding, in addition to adding transfers Wiley-Gatewood and Marrone. Wiley-Gatewood, who will become eligible at the end of the 2006 fall semester, was the starting point guard on then-No. 1 Tennessee and has tremendous natural instincts at the position. Marrone was a productive point guard in her one season at Virginia Tech, providing the Terps with an abundance of depth at a position where they were thin during the title run.

Maryland's talent pool likely will increase as Frese continues to work her magic on the recruiting trail. Success didn't slow the coach over the summer. She traveled across the country in pursuit of the nation's best young players, and it's obviously much easier to sell a program coming off a national championship season than a 10-18 year.

While the optimism is justified, Frese is aware of the tenuous nature of NCAA Tournament play. The Terps went into overtime twice in their six tournament games, and two others weren't decided until the final minutes. The margin between victory and defeat is razor thin, but Maryland has the talent to widen the margin next season. There is every reason to believe the team's chemistry again will be the key factor in its success, but that means the players must again check their egos.

The Terps got an early jump on their title defense with a May trip to Europe. Maryland went to four countries — France, Hungary, Austria and Czech Republic — in 12 days and played four games. They were 3-1, their only loss coming in overtime in a game that neither Newman nor Doron played in. After a long season, the trip was as much about enjoying the different cultures of Europe as it was about competition.

In an attempt to get a deserved rest, Frese and much of her family took a trip to Las Vegas, where her desire to see Celine Dion in concert was thwarted when the singer was stricken by a stomach virus similar to the one that hit Maryland in Albuquerque. Fortunately for Terps fans, Frese and her players weren't stopped by such setbacks.

In Central City, Ky., the local Wal-Mart started selling University of Maryland jerseys and was reportedly preparing a sign that proclaimed itself to be the hometown of Jade Perry, national champion.

Toliver continued to grow more comfortable on the public stage and even served as grand marshal of Harrisonburg's Fourth of July parade.

Sometimes the fulfillment of a dream doesn't live up to the expectations, but that wasn't the case for the Terps. The significance and emotion of the accomplishment exceeded anything they had imagined. For many of the players, the title run vindicated their decision to attend Maryland. Langhorne vividly recalls some of the game's most prominent coaches telling her she would never get to a Final Four, much less win a national title, if she became a Terp.

As much as the Terps were fueled by their perceived lack of respect during the season, it was merely a motivational ploy. There is no "I told you so" tone in their voice, just an appreciation for what they accomplished and the hope that there is more to come.

"We are more like a family than a team," Coleman said. "I know after we graduate, this team will keep in touch — that's how close we are. Looking at pictures [from the tournament] are the best memories. My mom has about a million newspapers and I was looking at them — just seeing the emotion on our faces [was the best part]. Those are some of the best memories ever, and you feel the emotions of [the championship] game. It's a feeling I hope we get a few more times."

ABOUT THE AUTHORS

Chris King, a sports writer for more than 12 years, has covered men's and women's college basketball extensively, spending countless hours on campuses and press rows across the country. Currently a staff writer for the Terrapin Times, King gained a unique view of the 2005-06 Maryland women's team as it developed into a national champion. King and his wife Amy and son Cooper reside in Bel Air, Md.

Brenda Frese is the most dynamic young coach in women's college basketball. She took over the struggling Maryland basketball program in 2002 and four years later led the Terrapins to the NCAA national championship. Frese's relentless work and charisma on the recruiting trail have attracted some of the nation's top talent to College Park and helped position her to be the game's next coaching star.